Be Here As You Are

ZEPHYRA VUN

 FriesenPress

One Printers Way
Altona, MB R0G 0B0
Canada

www.friesenpress.com

ISBN
978-1-03-831860-2 (Hardcover)
978-1-03-831859-6 (Paperback)
978-1-03-831861-9 (eBook)

1. BIOGRAPHY & AUTOBIOGRAPHY, PERSONAL MEMOIRS

Distributed to the trade by The Ingram Book Company

To my late mom and dad.

To my unborn child.

To the cycles that connect them.

TABLE OF CONTENTS

Your sole purpose in life is to show up,

fully present and fiercely authentic,

to each and every moment.

Introduction : Journeying . . .

To make life one giant flow state has been my chosen purpose since 2019. This book is a chronological retelling of how my life unfolded after making that monumental decision. The wisdom I gained, the intuition I cultivated, and the depth at which I was able to connect with my true self, all of it came from a commitment to the singular act of being present. This book spans four years of deliberate living, of finding presence and flow, every day.

For me, flow is about being so completely and utterly present that a deep immersion into connectedness occurs. It is a heightened level of connection that is native only to the present moment. Its rich and expansive sense of oneness reminds us of what deep connection feels like in a world where it is scarce.

Flow stimulates a connection within the self and beyond the self. It bridges internal and external, or *self* and *other*. In this way, flow embodies non-duality—a unification of two entities where the definitive boundaries of each dissolve (self and other, you and an activity, mind and body, past and future, space and time, "good" and "bad"). In flow, separateness disappears.

As an intriguing result, the actions taken within a flow state release from them conditions and limitations. A state of flow is both non-dual and non-conditioned. Things just are as they are, with no consequential counterparts to them. This is because everything is simply, and constantly, unfolding in the now, a vast and infinite space of pure possibility. One thing is not dependent on another because dependency dissolves when duality dissolves. Again, things simply *are* as they are in each passing moment.

Flow is often described as "getting lost in the moment," which is a woefully accurate use of vocabulary. We feel *lost* in this magical state of being because it is unfamiliar; so different from our everyday existence where duality, conditions, and limitations take charge.

The question I continuously ask myself, then, provides a foundation for this book: If flow states are born from living in the here and now, creating condition*less* and deeply connective states of being, how can we demystify them so that they are not just rare, momentary experiences in which we feel *lost* and without bearings, but rather, natural home bases where we feel grounded and safe? Ones we can access as readily as the present is pervasive. For if the present moment (the breeding ground for flow) permeates everywhere and every*when*, why cannot flow itself?

My fascination with flow began not so much as a developed interest, but as a sudden necessity. In the summer of 2019, while juggling six jobs (one of which was the executive director of a brand-new non-profit organization, which in and of itself was equivalent to three jobs—so, nine—nine jobs), I reached a breaking point in my life, an acute physical and mental breakdown in my early thirties. It was a thirty-two-year culmination of pushing myself way too hard, ignoring my body and intuition, and people-pleasing to the extreme, detrimentally confusing external validation with internal desire. This led to (high-functioning) depression, anxiety, and even further confusion.

I believed, my entire life, that what others expected of me was my purpose. It drove me forward, steered my life's direction, was the fuel for my engine, and whatever other car metaphor you can think of. My deepening confusion came from the fact that what I wanted and what was expected of me were indistinguishable. In fact, I earnestly believe that if I had not been pushed to my shattering breaking point the way I had in 2019, this confusion would have been embedded to the point of no return. It would have matured from an adopted belief into an engrained truth—that my self-worth was dependent on what others expected of me. A measure of value so many of us unfortunately use, depend on, and suffer from, knowingly or unknowingly.

Allow me, for a moment, to explain how confusing and reality-skewing this can actually get. Your intrinsic motivations are the things that internally drive you. Typically, they are reflective of inner desires, your innate subjectivity, your innermost self. But sometimes, especially if others' requirements of you pilot your life throughout your formative years, your intrinsic motivations can be shaped, solidified, and perpetually reinforced by external expectation and validation.

I was genuinely driven and motivated by what others expected of me. What I (thought I) wanted equalled what others wanted *of* me. And until the age of thirty-two, I really did not know the difference.

This is, unfortunately, not uncommon. Something as ubiquitous as living in civilized society demands that we follow certain rules, standards, and expectations. Add on top of that things like culture, family, and religion and you can begin to see how easy, automatic, and inevitable it is to live a life *purposed* by expectation and rules. We lose our ability to know the difference between internal and external, between what we *want* to do and what we *should* do. ("Should" is a conniving little word that directs much of our lives, implying reference to the future and the past, but in actuality does not even exist in the present. We will revisit this idea later.)

Suffice it to say, I was confused. Prior to my breakdown, I think I genuinely thought I liked working nine jobs, but at the same time felt very unfulfilled. I was restless and unhappy but unable to identify exactly why that was the story of most of my twenties. My body knew, but I was so detached from it, I failed to see. Because it is when we favour the mind (a necessity for rule-following) that we somehow forget about and ignore our bodies, which inevitably leads to a focus on *doing* over *being*, and *thinking* over *feeling*.

A perfect example of this is how I coped with my father's passing. In May 2005, a month before my eighteenth birthday, my dad died very suddenly from an unforeseeable brain aneurism. It was an unfathomable, devastating event that I never really grieved. It happened just a few months before I was to embark on a six-year Master's of Architecture degree, which provided me with the ultimate coping mechanism. I buried myself in work instead of feeling my pain. Replacing any shred of *feeling* with high-pressure *doing* was certainly not hard given the copious amounts of work and demanding, late-night hours involved in studying architecture. It engrained in me a pattern of working to avoid feeling, then working harder to feel even less.

This life of laser focus was not new to me. From around six years of age, I engaged in multiple, competitive activities—gymnastics, jazz, ballet, modern dance, and piano. I excelled at all of them. So, naturally, to nurture my talents, I cumulatively practised and trained for these activities at least twenty hours per any given week throughout all of elementary school, not including various competitions and recitals. I often ate dinner in the car after school on the way to an activity, leaving one just a little bit early to arrive at the next one just a little bit late, becoming all too familiar with "power naps" and experiencing severe "Sunday scaries" by the first grade.

This is what ultimately seeded the aforementioned confusion—the one between inner desires and external expectations. When you are a child, what you are told to do is often mistaken for what you want to do. It is no surprise that, come adulthood, the two become enmeshed. We are *unconscious to our lives*, obeying a robotic routine devoid of real feeling, instead of *conscious within them*. Liveliness and embodiment wane because your life is led by some thing or someone that is not you.

Fast forward to the peak of my breakdown— approximately twenty years after finally slowing my impossibly busy adolescent lifestyle and fourteen years after starting architecture school (just to give you some idea of the lasting affect compounded expectation has on a person), I had to take a good, deep look at myself. My health, happiness, and life itself depended on it.

I pressed *pause* (or perhaps *stop* is more appropriate) on every single aspect of my life because a mental breakdown is completely incapacitating. You simply cannot function, at all. Temporarily cutting myself off from my job, my relationship, and my social life, I took this "free" time (for the most part around nature) to attempt to answer the following question: "What makes me happy?" It was a surprisingly difficult task. Unable to nail down an answer, I reworded the question slightly: "When do I feel the most fulfilled?" The answer came almost immediately: when I am in flow.

Ever since this exact moment in time, I have dedicated myself to prioritizing my life around this feeling, this state of utter presence and effortless connection. It is a state I feel most when deep in a creative process making my art, or moving my body alongside others, coaching group fitness classes.

I share this personal history to expose the unawakened mind and body that I inhabited before setting off on this lifelong pursuit of finding flow. Perhaps it is relatable. I have come a long way since then, and the journey to where I am now can hopefully become relatable, too.

A few thoughts and disclaimers before continuing to share my story: this is not a how-to, nor a guidebook. It is a compilation of my own subjective experiences that I hope will spark a curiosity in examining your own. I am not here to lay out a set of rules for you to follow, nor specific causes to reach desired effects. On the contrary, I explore a state of mind and being that allows you to adapt and shift fluidly in your life so that you no longer need to rely on established rules, nor cause and effect. Rather, you can invent your own "rules" organically and create from what's inside instead of reacting to what's outside.

I wholeheartedly believe in the sentiment "show, don't tell." I believe it is more effective to lead and live by example than to lay out directives for others to follow. This is why I question the viability of the current "self-improvement movement" and the recent surge in self-help programs—particularly ones that suggest adhering to a set of steps or standards will grant a specific outcome. Quite frankly, it insults the uniqueness of an individual soul to claim that an objective number of steps or a specially curated list of tricks cannot only guarantee results, but the same results for everyone. It is presumptuous and generic, and it further perpetuates society's reliance on—and endorsement of—uniformity and expectation, which is ironically what these self-help programs are often attempting to dismantle. "Rediscover your true self by following these five simple steps!" "Ten tricks to establishing your unique values!" They use the very same binary, cause-and-effect structure (follow x and you'll get y) to help you achieve something different and better than what that same structure previously promised.

It is important to remember that our tendency to believe these self-help claims (follow x and you'll get y) is not our fault. We were raised to think and approach life exactly in this way. This book, therefore, will undoubtedly bring up questions, will implore you to reflect and rethink, revealing the profound influence of our inherited belief systems. So, despite being brought up on the notion that fulfillment is linked to what can be attained via an expected, rule-following path, I invite you to suspend that default mode of judgement and open yourself up to unfamiliarity, the unexplainable, and the provocative unknown as you explore the ensuing pages.

We would do well to implement a "beginner's mind," the Japanese Zen concept of approaching something with zero knowledge. It is confronting the unknown with the naiveté of a child, freshly receptive without any preconceptions or biases. It is a powerful practice of simplicity, surrender, and acceptance that optimizes learning and growth. Allow my words to speak for themselves instead of trying to do that job for them. For once, try not to think so hard. (And notice how often you do.)

Finally, I would be remiss not to mention a little something called quantum physics. It is the study of existence at the most fundamental level, in the realm of atoms and electrons. This quantum realm behaves in very peculiar ways compared to our physical one. For example, measurable energy drastically outnumbers measurable matter in the quantum realm. Each and every atom in the quantum realm encompasses a massive energy field whose size hugely exceeds that of its nucleus (considered matter), implying that our physical reality is actually more nonphysical than physical (more energy than matter). Also, the unpredictable behaviour of electrons, in wave or in particle form, seems to be influentially structured by an observer, as in the simple act of observing can influence reality. (Apparently, an observer of a quantum physics experiment can alter the state of an electron from a wave to a particle function, or vice versa, just by focusing attention on it. This is called a "quantum event," or "observer effect.")[1] These discoveries suggest a nonphysical, nonlinear existence—one that is absent of linear space and time or any kind of comprehensive cause-and-effect, pragmatic framework. Consequently, it is in the quantum realm where they say manifestation occurs. It is suggested that by cultivating a sense of presence, setting an intention, and aligning with the right frequencies, we are able to observe and manifest (just like electrons) certain wants, needs, desires, and outcomes, attracting them to us by accessing the quantum realm. In other words, the present moment is deemed the access point to the quantum realm and manifestation.

I only know any of this because during the time of writing this book I was reading quite extensively on topics varying from quantum physics, philosophy, neuroscience, intuition studies, and the like. I give you this very brief, grossly overgeneralized quantum lesson for two reasons. One, because it is within this field of study, the one that examines the very building blocks of life, that uncovers the experiential phenomena of *the present moment*—the place where energy is abundant, the place where time and space disappear, and the place where the focus of this book squarely lands. Two, because it is a science. Quantum physics is (just like any other objective, scientific field of study) based on provability through empirical measurement, the search for the known. Comparatively, spirituality is based on devoted trust in the unknown. Historically, scientific endeavour tends to compete with spiritual endeavour. Why does this matter?

Quantum physics contributes to the study of presence and of basic existence, yes. It offers a fact-based window into an elusive world. A world that is nonlinear, where there is no compulsory cause and effect, nor limitations of time and space—much like the world I empower the reader of this book to discover and create for themselves. However, I devote only a handful of paragraphs to it, because while quantum physics has its highly credible place, I feel it proves the wrong point here, which is that there is even a point to be proven at all.

Science aims to prove and convince, while the aim of this book is to offer experiential insight. (Is one more valuable or important than the other? Why? From where does our constant need to *prove* stem? Why is it so hard to simply *trust*? These are all intriguing questions I will attempt to address throughout this book.) Science tries to eradicate uncertainty, while spiritual belief (of any kind) honours and respects it. I believe the necessity to prove diminishes the merit of trust.

In Part One you will be introduced to *trust* as an integral aspect to living with purpose in the present. I will propose that trust, by definition, requires uncertainty, and when that uncertainty is removed, trust becomes knowledge. Consequently, when we are constantly driven to prove and to know, there is no longer a need for trust.

Therefore: Because trust is such an important piece to presence, intuition, and flow (as you will read in the proceeding section), and because trust requires a level of uncertainty to even be considered trust at all, I present a limited glimpse into quantum physics here as an avenue to further pursue, at your own discretion, to potentially expand your breadth of understanding on the topic of presence and manifestation—but one that I am personally choosing to put less emphasis on simply because *trusting* has led me to experience more deep meaning in life than *proving* ever will.

PART ONE : BE

If flow is a place of presence, intuition is the language of that place.

I wrote that phrase in my journal around the same time I was experiencing a swell of insightfully revelational dreams, a regular occurrence in my life. One dream in particular was about a waterslide, a dream that I knew upon waking needed to be decoded. I will delve deeper into this decoding in the paragraphs to follow, but first I want to speak about two keys I have found integral to *be*ing, to living in the here and now. Those two things are *clarity* and *trust*. I believe they are the foundations we must consciously lay in order to *be*—to live with presence, and therefore with purpose. Without a genuine curiosity, understanding, and active cultivation of clarity and trust, whatever good habits and well-intentioned efforts that follow will not have solid ground on which to stand. Consequently, clarity and trust are also prerequisites to unlocking flow.

Clarity and Trust

Clarity is unencumbered awareness. It is synonymous with expansion of the mind and body. It requires a couple of things: an acknowledgement and a release (in that order) of conditioned beliefs that no longer serve the self. To become clear means to release old thoughts and feelings that cloud our present existence, which form our present awareness. In this way, clarity requires regression before progression, or unlearning then relearning. One must regress to the state of mind of their innocent, open-minded, inner child in order to relearn and reform themselves with a clearer lens. And not just once, but again and again. It is a continuous, reiterative process that first involves the initial recognition of attachment to expired beliefs (an often monumental, life-altering realization or event. See Introduction), followed by the subsequent (and consistent) upkeep of culling and release. Without ridding ourselves of a past that has already served its purpose, clarity cannot be achieved. Another way to think of it is: attachment to the past is an obstacle for clarity.

Unfortunately, far too often, we fail in this. We remain attached to the past, resisting letting go, whether consciously or not. This makes us more and more susceptible to, and dependent on, attachment—holding on for dear life to what we already know. It means associating with our minds so much that we *become* these (limiting) thoughts and beliefs—those that have been stored in the mind for far too long, the ones that rely on our very attachment to them to remain viable. Cultivating clarity therefore both requires and facilitates *non*-attachment. Clarity is the consistent act of letting go to keep our path clear, not stuck in the past (nor worried about the future, for that matter), but aligned with the present. By virtue, clarity *is* presence.

Those who are narrow-minded lack true clarity. Their beliefs, values, and therefore self-worth have been shaped and concretized by *expectation* (what we already know), a symptom of living in the past and/or future. This is a rampant and cyclical system. Narrow-minded people believe what is expected and expect what they already believe. This becomes a sealed loop of closed-mindedness that feeds a reliance on external validation. For how can one validate oneself if one's self-worth is inextricably linked to external expectation—if your value comes from without instead of from within?

Perhaps an example would be helpful. In Western culture, many people believe that they are *expected* to live a heteronormative, monogamous life (having only one romantic partner of the opposite sex). This standard is bred from the past and dictates the future. It is "how things have always been done" and therefore should continue to be done. It is what we already know and is familiar. This well-established (societal, cultural, economical . . .)

expectation can easily become adopted as a personal belief; that heteronormative monogamy *should* be the compulsory way of engaging in relationships. If someone is closed-minded (attached to the past), their value becomes tied to this external expectation, this "should" condition. They may only feel worthy if they do what is expected and live a heteronormative, monogamous lifestyle. (Note: this is completely different from internally desiring heteronormative monogamy. Though, recall from the introduction that internal and external can often become indistinguishable without conscious self-awareness.) Conversely, if that person is able to find clarity by releasing attachment to "how things have always been done," disassociate from it, and widen their perspective to embrace validation from within, those external expectations will not hold so much weight. They will be able to choose based on personal values and beliefs, not involuntarily inherited ones.

I spent almost two years exploring ethical non-monogamy, or ENM. It was a beautifully open and radical space to negotiate the desires I was discovering and the expectations I was unravelling, simultaneously. I will make reference to some of these experiences throughout this book, as they played a pivotal role in my self-awakening.

The second key to living in the here and now is *trust*. Trust follows clarity and becomes more robust overtime. With a clear, open mind, trust builds on trust. The more times you experience trust in something, the more you are going to naturally trust it. This means an initial "leap of faith" ignites trust, and the continual, repetitive practice of leaning into vulnerability keeps it going. This is precisely why clarity must come first. If your mind is preoccupied with expectation, with the past or with the future, taking that initial leap of faith will be near impossible, because expectation (attachment to said past or future) is about *knowing*, not *trusting*. Though they may be synonyms in the dictionary, *knowing* and *trusting* are profoundly different.

When we expect something, we chase the certainty of it. Taking a leap of faith is the opposite of chasing certainty in the same way that living in the moment is the opposite of attachment to the past or future. While one depends on a level of uncertainty (trust), the other abhors it (expectation). Trust can therefore be incredibly difficult to practise and master. Having faith that what needs to happen will happen can seem like an outlandish concept, especially to twenty-first-century-bred neurotics. It is my belief that this challenge in trusting comes not so much from a person's conscious unwillingness to try, but rather the unconscious conditioning we collectively experience.

It is important to emphasize this inevitable blockade in cultivating trust: the unconscious conditioning we all undeniably experience growing up in a rule-based society. Recall that before trust, clarity must come—a release of established ways of thinking (or rules) that no longer serve a (good) purpose. It is imperative that trust come from this release, and not simply from the planting of a new seed. In other words, trust cannot simply be learned. It must be built up from that process of *un*learning and *re*learning; that process we have already named: clarity.

So: Trust means to recognize the inherent uncertainty of the act itself and still believe. Clarity facilitates trust by lending it an expansive, present space within which to be seeded and grow. Together, they give unbridled access to flow and intuition, the language of the present.

Flow and Intuition

If flow is a place of presence, intuition is the language of that place. Around the same time of jotting down this phrase in my journal, I dreamed of a waterslide. It was an unusually wide one, perhaps twenty feet or even wider. In the dream there was no stream of water running down the slide, which prevented me from using it. In my dream state, I discerned that the onus was on me to pour buckets of water down this massive slide in order to make traversing it even possible. I felt an unusually strong motivation to undertake this seemingly trivial responsibility.

I awoke from this dream *knowing* there was a message hidden within, one that would arouse deeper meaning in the instinctive words written in my journal. With the aforementioned thoughts of clarity and trust taking up critical space in my mind at the time as well, the following formula flowed from my pen in a free-flow writing exercise:

CLARITY + TRUST = FLOW + INTUITION

Zephyra Vun

How I deciphered this in relation to my dream, like unravelling the clues to a puzzle with unexpected ease, was as follows:

> *Clarity* = The expansion or widening of the waterslide. The ability to exist in the present, unattached to past or future.
>
> *Trust* = The repeated action of pouring water down the waterslide. The priming of the channel for use and reception.
>
> *Flow* = The water itself. The stream of materialized presence.
>
> *Intuition* = What comes down the slide with the water, the reception of which trust enables.

In the context of my journal entry, intuition is the language or the messages we want to receive from being in a place of presence (what comes down the waterslide with the water). With a foundation of clarity and trust, a state of presence can more readily manifest, from which intuition will naturally flow. As the dream revealed, the onus is on each of us to make dutiful efforts in attentively preparing this place to effectively hear and understand the language—to open our minds and our hearts, widening the waterslide that is our purview, and to repeatedly prime our own channels of present awareness with the water that is trust in order to receive intuitive messages with which to align ourselves.

Though this may seem inconsequential to the far-reaching purpose of our lives, I believe that this is exactly that—our purpose.

Purpose

When we think of the term "purpose," we may automatically turn to a personal passion or driving force unique to an individual's interests and intrinsic motivations. (Or sadly, sometimes extrinsic ones if we are not self-aware, as described in the introduction). For the most part, we think of purpose as something that brings our life meaning and that sustains our being. While this definition is true, I am referring to it here as a deeper, underlying force that is common across humanity as opposed to something that distinguishes us. While it remains true that an artist's purpose may be different from that of a doctor, or a mother's from that of a stranger, the way in which I refer to *purpose* here reaches beyond identification and representation. It cuts through the (many, complex) layers that define our character, our roles, and what we do in life, to the very depths—perhaps very bottom—of who we are; our truest nature as humans. Regarding purpose in this way simplifies it. Not in the sense that it removes meaning, but removes what does not matter, and on the contrary, *gives* meaning. Removing superficiality, looking beyond the surface of what is expected of us, our purpose is no longer a question of *what we do* but *who we are* in every waking, present moment. For *this* is where the most real and authentic versions of ourselves reside.

Philosophical? Yes. Radical? You bet. Complicated? No. In fact, our purpose is quite simple. Clarity and trust are quite simple. Perhaps not so much in their initial practice and execution, but certainly in their essence. To be uncomplicated is to find clarity. To let go and just be is to trust. And the richness of flow and intuitive wisdom that follow are also the purest, most natural, *simple* forms of being and consciousness.

To illustrate this simplicity, here is a dot.

●

"BE"

That is all you need to know for now. In the pages to follow we will build on this diagram, offering a simple visual of how life can become unnecessarily cloudy and disconnected when we stray too far from this grounding reference point of simply *be*ing.

PART TWO : HERE

As long as you are here, you can flow anywhere.

Middle Existence

There is an elusive space that aligns us with our intuitive flow. A space that some say bridges what we consider real and mystical. In this space, we exist between the past and the future, and also between the physical and metaphysical. This space is the present, the here and now.

The present is elusive only because we label it as such. This misguided label, the way we perceive the present, makes it very difficult to "live in the moment." Labels like "past," "present," and "future" become distinct points of reference for our lives. To envision it, we see a singular, minuscule point (the present) between two infinitely long, horizontal lines on either side (past and future). To live presently, still, in this "middle existence," seems daunting and near impossible when we perceive time and life as forward-moving on a linear trajectory.

Not only does the present exist at the seemingly minuscule point between past and future, but also between the physical and metaphysical. While the physical world is tangible, the metaphysical world encompasses all that is beyond what is perceptible to the five senses. The metaphysical transcends (what our limited human brains deem as) "reality." One might say a house, a pair of shoes, and my cat are physical, while energy, thoughts, and love belong to the metaphysical.

The here and now straddles these four worlds—past, future, physical, metaphysical. For this reason, the present is at once the most real and mystical thing. It is real because it makes up each moment of the human experience. No one can argue the palpability of the present moment. It is mystical because it defies measurability. Like energy, thoughts, and love, it belongs to a realm of existence that we cannot see or prove objectively. Its provability relies on belief and feeling, not seeing and calculating.

There are zero limitations or expectations in the present. *Shoulds* and *ifs* do not exist here. Unlike the past, the future, and the physical world, the present has no boundaries— hence why its existence reaches beyond what is quantifiable into what is deemed mystical. Unlike the past and the future, both of which have compartmentalized edges defined by *before* now or *after* now, the *here* and now defies these quantitative restraints. The here and now is constantly in flux, changing, evolving, and undefined, much like the flow of water. It is *pure, uninhibited, inclusive existence.* In comparison, *shoulds* and *ifs* are inhibiting and exclusive, drawing a line through existence where *x* fits on this side of *should* or *y* fits on that side of *if,* emphasizing separateness. *Shoulds* and *ifs* exist only in the past or the future, never the present.

To overcome separateness, to live in this middle existence of pure, uninhibited, inclusive presence is incredibly expansive and connective. Allow me to expand on the graph introduced earlier:

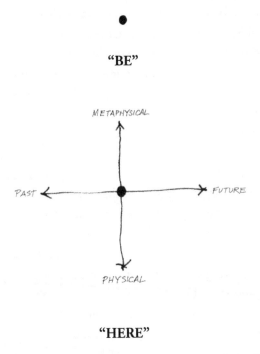

"BE"

"HERE"

With the addition of crossed lines, this iteration of the dot suggests that when we situate ourselves here, in the middle, we are able to expand outward in multiple directions from that middle point of reference. While our physical bodies are grounded in the "real world," we simultaneously connect beyond the physical into where intuition and flow (both transcendent experiences) can be accessed. While here, we may also begin to entertain the notion that past and future collapse with deep presence; that there really is no such thing as past nor future, but only present. For, like water or energy, that dot representing "middle existence" is never stagnant and is continuously evolving into the next moment. Being *here* means moving with this constantly emerging flow. Remaining here means there is no existential point of reference other than the one you are in now. You become one with this middle existence, and nothing exists outside of it/you. Your physical body moves with the metaphysical creation of each present moment, and as the diagram depicts, existence is no longer linear, but multi-directional and multi-dimensional, radiating infinitely outward. Instead of going down a linear path where there is a definitive beginning (toward the past) and end (toward the future), we can begin to experience existence, and therefore time, as rippling outward. This understanding allows you to actually shape how you feel time. It feels less like a forward-moving passage of seconds and minutes that inevitably slip away and more like an expansive opening, an autonomous creation of what is in front of you, now. Quite literally, to be *here* means not just living presently, but *becoming* presence. You *are* here.

This may seem like a foreign concept. We were neither taught nor encouraged to understand, never mind *live* in this space. The very nature of the way we accept and function within our *should*-driven modern environments is certainly not conducive to a pure, uninhibited space like the present. I say "modern" because I suspect it was not always this way . . . .

It is my belief that Western civilization's interest in studying the mind, the birth of psychology, and the constructed interpretation of the ego shifted focus from the body (a vessel for intuition) to the mind (a conjurer of past and future) and consequently established their separateness. As in, not only was the mind assumed more important than the body during this evolutionary time, but also completely separate from it. It is also my belief that this concept of separateness, the opposite of a connective "middle," instigated that which would become the *root cause* of our ensuing disconnection, within ourselves and from others. "Othering," or defining through separation, or thinking in black and white terms, is the fundamental reasoning behind all suffering, a.k.a. our lack of ability to *be here, to be present.*

Recall that being present is connective (as illustrated by the last diagram). It is the middle between past, future, physical, and metaphysical, wherein you *become* the space within which you exist (you *are* here). "Othering," or binary thinking (a term with which you will become very familiar), is our default mode of awareness when we fail to do this. In other words, the present is the only place where your physical body and the space in which you inhabit overlap and become one. So, to exist anywhere outside of this place is to separate from everything else that is not you (other), and to live in binary terms. The vast majority of us exist outside this place.

The concept of binary thinking or binary existence (terms I will use interchangeably going forward) is a particularly important one to understand. There is an entire section to follow dedicated to it, for as I said earlier, it is precisely the concept of binary thinking that is the root cause (and effect!) of separateness, of "othering," and of living *outside* the diagrammatic dot that is present, middle existence.

Binary thinking is omnipresent yet nearly undetectable (unless you make the conscientious effort to become aware of it). It is our automated, programmed mode of existing. How we perceive, how we function, and the decisions we make are all, for the most part, binary in nature. It is so ubiquitous that we rarely think about it or identify with it.

Here is a list of paired entities. The list as it is written is reflective of how we think of each pair in typical, binary terms.

> Self or Other
>
> Body or Mind
>
> Past or Future
>
> Certainty or Vulnerability
>
> Monogamy or Non-monogamy
>
> Internal or External
>
> Good or Bad
>
> Intuition or Intellect

Each part of the pair is separate, defined by its own boundaries. One is not the other, as identified by the word *or*. For the sake of simplicity, we will use this list throughout this section, but beyond these eight examples is virtually any two things you can think of, because of the fact that we automatically and unanimously think, and therefore exist, via separation. We like to put things in boxes because compartmentalization is how we understand. If it doesn't fit in this box, then it must belong to some *other* box. This mindset is unconscious and universal.

The last pair in the above list is especially compelling, particularly in how it directly applies to what has been already discussed. I isolate this pair and digress for a moment because it contextualizes and bolsters the preceding ideas, embedding them in an intriguing philosophical question.

Intuition and intellect seem like opposite ends of the spectrum. While one is associated with the mystical body, the other is with the controlled mind. One may imply believing in a power beyond the self, while the other advocates for self-sovereignty. "Things are meant to be, and my intuition will take me there" versus "I intellectually make my own decisions that affect the outcome of my life" are also plausible conflicting mindsets that each might hold. But why is it that one is opposite, or even different from the other? Why must they exist in competition, vying for their own importance while, through process of elimination, rejecting the others'? The answer: because of binary thinking.

Binary thinking, or othering, wedges distance between two things and pits them against each other. As a result, the mere existence of one threatens the existence of the other. Seen as distinct, opposing forces, believing in some intuitive power greater than the physical self, for example, may *threaten* believing in the ability to employ intellect, and vice versa.

Without conscious self-awareness, this is how we exist. It is how we perceive, how we navigate the world around us, and how we understand ourselves through a lens of disconnection and detachment. The good news, if you recall, is that there is a place where binary existence dissolves (and *e*volves) into middle existence. That place is the present—the dot—being *here*.

In regards to the idea of intuition versus intellect, it is in the present moment, and in the present moment alone, that these two seemingly disparate beliefs inevitably collide. For as I stated at the beginning of this section, *the present moment is, at once, the most real and mystical thing*. It is in this vast space of radical possibility where what is "real" (arguably the intellect camp) and "mystical" (arguably the intuition camp) are no longer separate, nor threatening to each other. In the present, where binary thinking is vanquished, where conditions like *shoulds* and limitations like *ifs* have no place, middle existence assures that believing in a higher intuitive power is no different than believing in your intellectual self. They are no longer considered opposites but instead become one. You *are* that higher power.

Furthermore, it is worth asserting that higher power carries merit. But unfortunately it is a kind of merit that is rarely acknowledged. Because of the unprovability or immeasurability of intuition (the *language of the present*, as presented in Part One), we neglect its importance and credibility. In our logical, physical-focused world, any type of knowledge that cannot be empirically proven does not receive much attention. Binary thinking further amplifies this belief by othering intuition and intellect, by enforcing their oppositeness, where the validity of one consequently erases the validity of the other.

This is pertinent to what was discussed in the introduction, the case of science versus spirituality, or our incessant need to use objective research to prove something.

By embracing the merit of intuition, one could argue that whatever quantum physics is trying to prove about the present (in regards to spiritual and manifestation practices) can and has already been proven many times over, just in a different way—through subjective experience rather than objective science. Spirituality existed long before quantum physics. But when you stack something one intuitively knows and experiences against something derived from a laboratory test, the latter is always deemed more credible. While not surprising, I think it is important to acknowledge the profound value of the former, which simultaneously advocates that some things simply cannot (and should not) be explained. Respect for the unknown and acceptance for the magic and mystery of life should be enough.

Another pair in the list of entities that I personally find interesting is that of monogamy or non-monogamy. One could argue that these two are distinct opposites. One means having only one partner, and the other means having multiple. While I do not disagree that they are different, I would challenge the notion that they are opposites. The plain fact that our minds automatically go to that place and deem them as such is telling of our fixed, binary way of thinking.

Having purposefully immersed myself in the world of ENM, I can say from experience that the two are not as black and white as one might presume, and there can be overlap and fluidity between the two. To illustrate this more clearly, here is a (very limited, and random) list of definitions and ENM vocabulary with which I became quite familiar (both out of curiosity and necessity—Learning a brand-new way of living requires learning the language that goes along with it).

Polyamory: The practice of engaging in multiple romantic relationships with the consent of all involved. (This is the ENM practice I chose to engage in.)

Hierarchical Polyamory: A form of polyamory where certain romantic relationships are deemed more important than others, and therefore certain partners are prioritized over others (usually by employing *primary*, *secondary*, and *tertiary* designations).

Prescriptive vs. Descriptive Hierarchy: Prescriptive hierarchies are ones that are explicitly named (e.g. a "primary" partner). Descriptive hierarchies are not necessarily named but undoubtedly exist due to the natural way relationships function (e.g. sharing more emotionally with one partner over the other because you have been together longer, or syncing schedules only with the partner you live with).

Nesting Partner: The partner with whom you cohabitate. This is the singular, common definition. Other implications of a nesting partners can look very different from one relationship to the other (e.g., a nesting partner could mean someone you share finances with, or someone who holds "primary" status, or someone you just live with but do not have a sexual relationship with).

Swinging: The practice of engaging in recreational sex with others, usually not for the sake of emotional or romantic connection. Swinging can be practised as a couple, an individual, or a group.

Mono-Poly: A relationship structure where one person identifies as polyamorous and the other identifies as monogamous.

Monogamish: A newer term that identifies a couple who are, for the most part, monogamous, but who occasionally engage in casual forms of ENM.

Notice how your head is spinning a bit, and perhaps judgement is beginning to creep in? Though not ideal, that is normal. To be presented with new words that describe new worlds overwhelms us because it challenges and threatens our existing beliefs. Sometimes to the point where we dismiss the legitimacy of these new worlds simply due to a lack of understanding—or perhaps more appropriately, an unwillingness to understand. But opening ourselves up to the unorthodox is the only way to stimulate clarity (which I defined in Part One as *unencumbered awareness,* or *to release old thoughts and feelings that cloud our present existence*). This does not mean forcing the adoption of views that do not align with your values, but it does mean questioning where those values come from in the first place, withholding judgement by genuinely listening to the perspectives of others, and recognizing that we are in fact able and allowed to revolutionize customs that we previously thought were fixed.

The point of sharing the above terms is less to debate the semantics of whether monogamy and non-monogamy can exist simultaneously and more to expose the expansive scope and rife grey area of the ENM world. These are just seven of myriad innovative terms that describe the various and diverse forms of what relationships *can* look like, as opposed to what they *should* look like. The extensive terminology affectively expresses the idea of possibility in relationship choice; that your relationships do not have to fit into the confines of one of two existing boxes pre-established by society's expectations and instead can be defined by your individual needs. They can actually defy the need for traditional labelling and can emerge from the desires of the people involved, not the prescriptions of the people looking in. The possibilities are endless because choices are formed by moving through the boundless present moment, instead of by what has been done in the set ways of the past.

Regardless if the previous two examples of non-duality ring true for you personally or not, I do think the capacity for middle existence to unify and blur boundaries is clear and justified. We are perfectly capable of wrapping our heads around this concept if we just accept it. How often do we actually do this? To accept something for what is instead of actively trying not to? It is in our nature to react, to lead a binary existence where "making sense" depends on the allocation of what can and cannot be proved, and where one box's hard edges always bump against another's. But why not choose to be in the present, where there are no boxes and therefore no need to react, where only possibility and acceptance reside? For this is the only place where earthly realities merge with the beyond, where the human experience becomes one with otherworldliness.

To put this into context, let's revisit the list of pairs once more. Here they are presented with more fluidity and less duality. Boundaries start to blur. With a simple shift in word selection, akin to the shift in consciousness we all have the capacity to make, we can begin to perceive the world in terms of how we relate and connect (*middle*) instead of how we differ (*binary*).

Self **becomes** Other

Body **inside** mind

Past **connects** Future

Certainty **by** Vulnerability

Monogamy **and** Non-monogamy

Internal **with** External

Good **nor** Bad

Intuition **is** Intellect

To take this one step further and fully reconcile duality, we can begin to actually define the pairs' integrative parts:

Self **becomes** Other = flow.

Body **inside** Mind = embodiment.

Past **connects** Future = presence.

Certainty **by** Vulnerability = growth.

Monogamy **and** Non-monogamy = autonomous relationship.

Internal **with** External = balanced living.

Good **nor** Bad = how things align with your values.

Intuition **is** Intellect

I began this section by stating that there is an elusive space that aligns us with our intuitive flow. As I have come to understand, it is also a space that unifies, blurs boundaries, and facilitates an expansion of the mind. It is *here*, within middle existence, that we can learn to be less resistant—a state that is fed by perceiving only through differentiation—and become more accepting—a state that sees past what separates us and is more open and receptive to that which connects.

Binary Existence
("If This, Then That")

The concept of binary existence (the opposite of middle existence) has been introduced. Before looking at some common examples of thought patterns that result from binary existence, I want to dissect the concepts of *binary* and *duality* a bit further in order to reveal just how deeply it is engrained in the human psyche and how tight a hold it has on each of us.

Computer coding relies on binary relationships, defined by two parts that are not the same. Infinite patterns of ones and zeroes (binaries) are used to create formulas—orders, if you will—for a computer to calculate and then execute. The computer understands that *if* a formula contains a specific pattern of ones and zeroes, *then* it is to perform x function. *If* it contains a different pattern, *then* it will perform y function. The formulas or commands are all separate and distinct from each other (binaries), as are the resulting functions (again, binaries). A one is not a zero, and *this* particular pattern of ones and zeroes and its resulting function is not *that* particular pattern of ones and zeroes and its resulting function. As we have come to realize by this point, we behave in a very similar way.

We are the ones who create these virtual realities and the machines in which they operate. And they reflect our physical, real ones. (Why wouldn't they? We made them.) Humans operate via the same binary formulas as the machines we create, and in turn, those machines generate and emit even more suggestive coding for us to follow (#algorithms.) The more technologically advanced we become, and the more our lives are influenced by, directed by, and dependent on machines, the more we surrender to, and rely on, our shared programming without much thought or effort. We become as unconscious as the digital machines we manufacture. So ubiquitous is this binary existence, it is difficult to identify the source. Who or what is responsible for our unconscious dependency on this binary existence? Enter: the ego.

The ego is the vehicle through which we navigate a binary reality. The ego, like a computer, uses an *if this, then that* formula to shape reality.

If you think back on the previous section, which introduced the basic definition of binary existence (essentially, understanding through separateness), consider *if this, then that* as the next step. It is putting the distinct separateness of the binary relationship into action, or putting parts into a whole. It is putting the aforementioned ones and zeroes into an actual formula. It is the ego attempting to decipher and compute the list of pairs from earlier (e.g. intuition and intellect).

The ego receives and inputs data from our surroundings, a theoretical series of ones and zeroes, to create and output a particular scenario for the self. *If* I go to university and obtain a degree, *then* I will be an intelligent, contributing member of society. *If* I get married and have children, *then* I will feel fulfilled. *If* I cry right now, *then* I will be perceived as weak. The series of ones and zeroes are endless, and there is always a consequence or condition attached to it. This also implies that no action, whether it is "this" or "that," can exist on its own without bearing on something else in the future (a.k.a. cause and effect). The ego says, "I cannot just cry for the sake of crying. *This* must mean *that*. Things cannot just be as they are. There needs to be an effect—a future outcome, consequence, or condition—attached to my cause."

This begins to define the very nature of *expectation*, a past-informed, future-driven mentality unique to humans. (Recall the monogamy example from Part One). As we navigate our binary world via a binary ego in this expectational way, we not only exacerbate separateness, but we repeat and engrain the same series of ones and zeroes, programming the same unwavering beliefs and realities. We constantly anticipate the same results. It is when we fail to remain curious and question the input (or the output, for that matter) with a critical eye—when we cease to seek novelty and shy away from vulnerability, becoming all too comfortable with what has already been coded—that the seemingly obvious difference between man and machine starts to vanish.

The ego, the switchboard of the psyche, is intuition's evil twin. While they are both guiding, inner voices, it is up to us to decide to which voice we pay more attention. Here are some contrasting ways in which each operate . . . .

EGO

- There is always a cause and an effect.
- You live by the ego's formula: "if this, then that."
- You perceive in terms of limitation and scarcity.
- You live *defensively*, *reacting against* and *preparing for* the *ifs* and *shoulds* of a past-informed, future-driven reality.

INTUITION

- Something just is for the sake of itself.
- You just live: "if this, ~~then that~~."
- You perceive in terms of possibility and abundance.
- You live *offensively, accepting* and *creating* what is right in front of you in each moment from a present reality.

To provide another iteration of the diagram with which we have started to become familiar, below are two examples of binary existence (a.k.a. non-middle existence, a.k.a. non-present existence, a.k.a. being *there* as opposed to being *here*). In this case, your existence no longer overlaps with the present, so the dot still represents the present, while the *x* now represents you.

The first example may represent an individual who obsesses about preparing for the future. They are overly cautious, overly reserved, or are always anticipating the worst-case scenario and exhibiting little to no trust (a worry-wart type). The second may represent someone who lives in the past. They are stubborn, attached to reliving and defining themselves through old memories or principles, hindering open-mindedness and clarity. Though different, both are examples of *not being* here—physically, mentally, spiritually. Their tunnel vision, whether backward- or forward-facing, prevents them from living in the now.

"THERE"

You will also notice that the physical and metaphysical *y*-axis are absent from this binary version of the diagram. This is because there is neither a physical nor mystical realm within a binary existence.

As perplexing as this sounds, as I have said before, what we perceive as confusing is usually just a result of our minds reacting to something unfamiliar. So, just listen: the past has already happened. The future has not happened at all. Neither are happen*ing* in the present so are neither real nor mystical (*y*-axis). There is zero existence in the past; there is zero existence in the future. Your body cannot exist in either. They are simply conjectures of the mind. So, a being who siphons their energy into either the past or future will always be living a linear (*x*-axis only), binary existence composed of a clear beginning, middle, and end, and nothing else.

This being chases down this linear path with blinders on to anything that deviates from it. (More on the idea of chasing in the next section.)

There are three main takeaways from examining this binary system, which we both rely on and produce. (We truly do create our own problems.) The first is that binary existence always involves cause and effect. Things cannot just be as they are. A cause must have an associated effect for something to make sense. There needs to be a reason, a contradiction, a consequence, a reaction . . . some revolving condition to complete the ego's equation.

The second is that validity, value, and acceptance are defined by objective provability. Binary thinking is black and white, good or bad, this or that. Because it is so precisely definitive, where one thing cannot be another, and is described with hard, categorical lines discounting any kind of grey area, binary thinking leaves no room for chance, possibility, uncertainty, the unknown. That which cannot be proven is left unvalued and unaccepted.

The factual truth is, we do not know everything. And to claim that we do, or to try so fiendishly, is reckless. There does not have to be a reason, nor an explanation, for all we experience—nor what others experience. But a binary existence insists on interpreting the world in this manner, in my opinion, to our detriment. To recognize and release this mode of awareness is liberating. It reveals just how and why the human experience is so fascinating and enables us to be more accepting—of ourselves and of others. When the need to prove or define no longer exists, all that is left is discovery and acceptance of what is.

The third takeaway, and perhaps the most defeating, is the polarity that binary thinking generates. Polarity is a direct symptom of the previous two takeaways combined, which has a blaring presence in today's reality. Because things cannot simply be as they are and are instead defined by structural cause and effect (a reason) and objective provability (an explanation for the reason), the space between the two parts of a binary relationship grows exponentially large. The differences are amplified and the disconnection between them reinforced. You believe in A and I believe in B, therefore we are not the same. You cannot objectively explain the reason why you believe in A, therefore I cannot accept or validate you. You believe in A, and I do not, then that must mean I believe in B, since there are only two (binary) options. We create a world of opposites and assumptions, where ideas and people are forcibly pitted against one another in an endless effort to explain their reason, to prove their cause and effect, rather than simply allowing, accepting, and honouring them to be as they are. We are currently stuck in this matrix where meaning must be quantified, resulting in honest expressions of individual selves becoming defined not by what they are but what they are not and, in doing so, becoming silenced for their uniqueness.

The inner self, the truest version of you that is most alive in the present moment, is obviously the greatest casualty in all of this. The reason it took me thirty-two years to uncover mine is becoming more and more clear. It is a revelation to wake up to our surroundings and to realize how much our own subjective reality is shaped by the one we all share.

Knowing this, would you not choose to exist in a reality that champions the inner self? A reality that rejects binary thinking, one that connects rather than separates? A present reality where you simply being creates purpose?

Though you have the ability to choose, I have learned that the act itself can be difficult. Not just in relation to *how*, but also to *what* and *why* we choose. In my experience, the journey of choice directly parallels the journey of moving up the consciousness ladder from binary to middle existence. Choosing or empowering choice is only possible when you move beyond living in the past or future to living in the present with purpose. Choosing is an act that is only as effective as how present you are. For me, this process of realization was marked by three stages.

Chase < Choose < Attract
(From Binary to Middle Existence)

The above three words are a selection of actions the self can take. As suggested previously, and as the lesser-than symbols (<) indicate, our adeptness at practising presence directly impacts our actions. I have found that chasing, choosing, and attracting are three significant turning points that denote a levelling up in that ability, as well as the ability to be efficient with our energy and attention. Moving through these stages is gradually learning the art of conserving energy to *attract* as opposed to losing energy to the *chase*. In the interim, we learn to *choose*.

As we have come to realize, when you live for the past or the future, you are not *here*, but over *there* somewhere. When you are not here, it is difficult to accept what is, and to trust, so you chase certainty and expectation instead. It feels safer because you are used to seeking validation from without, not from within. You chase said validation to fill the void that is left from you not being *here*.

This chase-mentality suggests two notable things. One, that you inherently lack something, and two, that you have no power in the matter. To *chase* inherently means that you are not only missing something, but that the obtainability of that something is out of your control. In other words, *lack* and *powerlessness* are inevitable symptoms of the chase mentality. Let's examine each one separately.

To believe that you inherently lack something is a direct result of binary, *if this, then that* thinking. As we have discussed, this mode of awareness creates separation (othering), duality, and consequence. Not only is one thing *not* the other thing, but *this* depends on its counterpart *that*, and vice versa. (Recall the ego's machine-like need to have a corresponding effect to any cause, a consequential *that* to *this*. Something cannot exist for the sake of itself. Cause and effect are paramount). *This* then often becomes the object of the chase, the thing we must obtain in order to achieve *that*. A prime and relatable example of this, as we have already seen, is the chase for the ideal, exclusive, monogamous partnership.

As previously suggested, within Western society, a non-present individual's worth and level of internal fulfilment can be tied to external attainment; in this particular case, the expectation of finding an exclusive, heteronormative, forever partner. To apply this situation to the *if this, then that* framework, the expectation computes: "If I find my exclusive life partner, then I will lead a fulfilling life," where *this* equals securing a monogamous, lifelong partner, and *that* equals a fulfilling life. Securing a monogamous, lifelong partner becomes the *cause*, the object of our chase, that will result in the desired *effect*: a fulfilling life. Without said cause (for example, remaining single, having multiple partners, prioritizing platonic relationships, not marrying, not committing for life), the desired effect (leading a fulfilling life) is unobtainable. What this spawns is the engrained belief that external attainment is the key to fulfillment; that we are lacking from the start, that we do not already have all that we need here and now. That we are not already whole.

Let's visualize this. Recall the comparison between the middle existence "HERE" and the binary existence "THERE" diagrams presented earlier in this section. In the former, time, space, and therefore existence radiate forever outward. In the latter, we move in one direction down a single line with a definitive end (spoiler alert, death). The former is an open state of being where internal worth is not dependent on external attainment (there is no cause and effect in the present, and therefore nothing to chase). The latter is narrow-minded and laser-focused on obtaining the object of the chase in order to be redeemed by an external source (the future, the monogamous partnership, *anything other* than you in the present). In the former, you choose from a state of wholeness. In the former, you chase from a state of lack.

If you have ever exercised any kind of gratitude practice, you will know how powerfully, yet simply, this state of lack can be transformed. When we express and harness gratitude for all that each present moment brings, as opposed to focusing on its inadequacy, devoid of everything that must yet be chased down, gained, or conquered in pursuit of the future, life will always feel full. This is how we stop chasing.

The second implication of the chase mentality is *powerlessness*. While chasing is the *result* of lack, it is both the result of and *reason* for powerlessness; i.e., "I am lacking, therefore I must chase *x*" versus "I am powerless, therefore I must chase *x*, plus the act of chasing itself perpetuates my feeling of powerlessness, because I cannot seem to capture *x*, and must continue chasing."

This is self-sabotage, a deep powerlessness that is augmented by societal conditioning and the ego. It is self-deprecation and defeat, and it comes from one main cause: you being a stranger to yourself.

This was revelational for me. The realization that when you do not know who you are or what you want, truly and unapologetically, *all* of your actions are going to be powerless chases, not empowered choices. All your actions are merely *re*actions to the outside world, not creations from within, as a direct result of not knowing yourself. This epiphany is how we make the transformational shift from chasing to choosing. Our selves become no longer defined by a sense of lack and powerlessness that can only be satiated by fulfilling expectation through external validation, but by our innate needs and desires, because we now finally know what those are. We tune in to our intuition, the voice that is already deeply familiar with those innermost needs and desires—but that some programming managed to suppress—and we finally align with our most authentic path.

Believing that choice is not only available to us in each and every moment, but that we are wholly deserving of it, is less celebrated than it should be. When we live unconsciously, we tend to see our lives as an accumulation of chases, of obligations that are outside of our control. But when we finally become conscious, we reach a breakthrough in self-actualization where we (re)discover who we really are and what we want. And from that renewed state of wholeness, when we realize that we are absolutely able and deserving of choosing, we awaken to a refreshed and empowered state of being. Our entire worldview shifts from being based on terms of probability to terms of possibility. From expectation to creation. Inevitably, our existence expands beautifully beyond earning, doing, and chasing to simply having, being, and choosing. All because you have, at last, arrived *here*.

This kind of life is a vulnerable one. You must enact acceptance and trust continuously, knowing that uncertainties lurk around every corner but choosing choice anyway. This is truly living presently. And as I mentioned before, being more efficient with our energy and attention comes as a result of this commitment. Therefore, the more present we are, the more intentional we are. We become more adept at setting boundaries and knowing when to say yes or no. This rigorous learning process is how choosing eventually becomes attracting, or manifesting.

In my experience, choosing is like the experimentation phase, and attracting is the actual execution. You must practise choosing, experiencing both failures and successes, in order to discover what it is that you want to attract. In other words, the conscientious act of choosing helps you narrow down what it is you desire to attract and manifest.

For me, choosing often looked like selecting what I *could* want, selecting what I could *compromise* for, or selecting what I wanted with certain *conditions*. But if the point is to truly and unapologetically hone in on our exact target of attraction, these hesitancies that surround our choices must be eliminated. By no surprise, this comes at the expense of our comfort. Exercising our willingness to say both yes and no is difficult and uncomfortable, especially if we are accustomed to someone or something else doing that job for us. However, once we lean into that empowering vulnerability, we reach the point where attraction actually becomes inevitable. For once you have chosen enough times and have eliminated the *coulds*, *compromises*, and *conditions*, the object of your attraction organically becomes clear, and everything else falls away. You eventually develop an intentional yet intuitive habit of saying yes to a highly curated list of things and no to everything else. Attraction is what I like to call energy-efficient choosing, which naturally paves its own trajectory through the process of elimination. Think about this logically: if you say "yes" to the things you do not truly want, you are actively inviting those things into your life. On the contrary, if you consciously hone in on what you want and commit to saying no to everything but, that is the power of attraction.

One can only choose, and eventually attract, if they commit to being *here,* physically, mentally, emotionally. If you find you are chasing, there is a good chance you are not present, not *here*, but over *there* somewhere. Two significant times in my life where I felt a consistent and genuine sense of being *here* was during a solo trip to Portugal in spring 2022, as well as throughout my commitment to exploring ethical non-monogamy at the onset of 2020. I believe both these experiences—while one was a period of weeks and the other years—provide relatable contexts in which to further explain how presence opens the doors to powerful experiences that call you to examine what you think you already know.

Portugal and Ethical Non-Monogamy

I realize this title may be suggestive of more seductive content than what is actually contained in this section of the book. To clarify, while my trip to Portugal and my almost two-year exploration in ethical non-monogamy were both *vast spaces of possibility* in which I was free to explore the unfamiliar (the very reason for including them in the book), they (alas) did not overlap.

In the spring of 2022, I took a month-long solo trip to Portugal. A month may not seem like a long time to seasoned travellers, but for me it was an exciting (albeit scary) opportunity to seek novelty, get inspired, and venture outside my comfort zone. The vast majority of Part One and Part Two of this book was written during this month of enrichment.

What I noticed almost immediately when I arrived in Lisbon was twofold: my uneasiness at being in a foreign country alone coupled with my unwavering commitment to staying present. "Just be here, Zeph. That's all you need to do" was what I kept repeating in my head anytime I would find myself in an expansive, destabilizing, uncomfortable or overwhelming situation, characteristic for a novice traveller such as myself. Taking in the breathtaking geography of the Douro Valley, making friends with suspect locals, the language barrier between my hostel landlord and I, getting lost on inebriated stumbles home at four a.m.—whatever the circumstance, a simple reminder to be *here*, in the present moment, somehow grounded me in whatever anxiety-provoking situation I found myself in. It was an embodiment, a felt understanding in the body more than a mental thought in the mind, that anchored me in the knowledge that I was *safe in the now*. It was an experience of deep trust through acceptance. An embodied trust that could only be felt by fully surrendering myself to the present, consciously accepting whatever the next moment brought with it, instead of catastrophizing the future. It was an unexpected, liberating feeling.

It only took a couple of days of finding my bearings in completely unknown territory to realize the words that begin Part Two of this book, *as long as you are here, you can flow anywhere*, which was one of the first sentences I jotted down in my travel journal. Translation: the present moment carries with it a natural certainty, one that is trustworthy as long as you *flow with it* and do not resist it. Finding anchorage here, despite whatever uncertainties surround you, is what creates a purposeful existence. In other words, as long as we are fully awake to the present, we are purposeful.

An integral element that facilitated this "forced" presence in Portugal was novelty. Experiencing something for the first time without any prior familiarity or expectation naturally pushes you into that *vast space of possibility that is the now.* You have no idea what is about to happen, nor do you ruminate on past memories, because there are none. It is a completely clean, unmarred slate from which you can design whatever experience you wish. This is not unlike the autonomy you encounter in ethical non-monogamy.

I could write an entire other book about my ENM experiences. Similar to my travels in Portugal, it was a time of immersing myself in completely unknown territory: in this case, deconstructing compulsory monogamy. (A reminder that it is the *compulsory* component of monogamy that can be problematic, not monogamy itself. It frames monogamy as the universal, unquestionably accepted and prescribed standard for relationships. The actual practice of monogamy, of having one, exclusive partner, is a personal choice that—like all other personal choices—should remain unjudged.) Imagine then having to examine this compulsory practice from all angles under a microscope, unlearning things you previously accepted as fact, then redesigning the definition of what a relationship is from that completely clean, unmarred slate. Imagine doing all this while others (who are close to you) judge you, question your motives, dismiss the validity of your choices, or naively but firmly decide that just because something is unrelatable that it is unacceptable. It would be a very long book.

Perhaps comparing the novelty of travelling to that of exploring a new relationship paradigm seems simplistic, but oftentimes simplicity gleans the most truth and insight. One blaring parallel I continuously draw between the two is that they both illuminate *process* instead of *outcome*. They emphasize the importance of a fluid existence that is malleable, created through trial and error, contrary to the black-and-white, all-or-nothing existence that is created through anticipated outcome; the one we so unconsciously and regularly fall into.

Because of ubiquitous binary thinking, we rarely think about the makeup of our lives in terms of processes, but rather, time-sensitive results. Certain achievements should be attained within a certain timeframe, just as things are either this or that, causes or effects. They are all consequences that we put into boxes defined by hard edges. If we are not careful, our entire life as a whole can be regarded as one giant outcome or consequence, defined by what *will* be, not simply by what *is* now. A *representation* of life, not a *way* of life. (The concept of living for retirement, for example, sacrifices presence and process for some distant future outcome that is far from guaranteed. This is an established societal standard). If we are not a part of or fully immersed in the process, all we see is the outcome, the representation, what will be. In order to lead a purposeful existence, we must immerse ourselves in the constantly evolving *process* that is now.

Thinking about existence as a process means that it is less linear and more cyclical. Think of a line compared to a circle. While one ends abruptly, the other's end seamlessly transitions into a new beginning. Unlike a linear structure, the completion of a cycle does not mean termination, but rather a renewed iteration. This is very important because it suggests that a cyclical, process-driven, expansive, middle existence requires something, an integral piece, that a linear, outcome-based, narrow-minded, binary existence does not. That integral piece is letting go.

Like a wave or a breath, letting go of the old is necessary for the creation of the new. A constantly evolving self is dependent on this act—one whose baggage and biased knowledge would otherwise be carried into the next moment on a linear timeline, compromising the capacity for renewed presence. This does not mean that we should not learn from past experience, but it does mean that we must be mindful that those past experiences do not interfere, command, override, or manipulate the present ones. The phrase "get out of your own way" comes to mind.

Applying this to the contexts of Portugal and ENM, a couple of takeaways are revealed. The first is that an outcome-driven existence, as in a chase-filled binary one (to use the terms expressed in the preceding sections), gives power to your past and future self, whereas a process-driven existence, as in a choice-filled middle one, gives power to the present self. A past and future self abide by customary rules because they derive known causes that will yield known effects, which ultimately help predict the future. A past and future self follow *the line* of expectation. A present self follows *the circle* of the present, abiding by what is relevant right now.

Dealing with language barriers and overall culture shock when travelling compels attention to what is relevant right now. The very words *barrier* and *shock* connote a sense of unfamiliarity, of novelty, where giving power to anyone but the present self would do a disservice to that self. We cannot expect anything in an unknown situation, so to desperately embed pre-acquired knowledge in an attempt to predict an unpredictable future is pointless. This is what I mean when I say we must be mindful that those past experiences do not interfere, command, override, or manipulate the present ones. Now, I realize this is a habitual human behaviour that makes us feel safe. Familiarity equals safety. But, as I proposed earlier in this section: *As long as you are here, you can flow anywhere . . . the present moment carries with it a natural certainty, one that is trustworthy as long as you flow with it and do not resist it.* In fact, the foundational inquiry of this book, stated in the first part of the introduction, aims at deconstructing this very concept:

If flow states are born from living in the here and now, creating conditionless and deeply connective states of being, how can we demystify them so that they are not just rare, momentary experiences in which we feel lost and without bearings, but rather, natural home bases where we feel grounded and safe? . . . Ones we can access as readily as the present is pervasive. For if the present moment (the breeding ground for flow) permeates everywhere and everywhen, why cannot flow itself?

This is a challenge with which I became well acquainted during my ENM days—this idea of cultivating presence through a conscious focus on what is relevant *now* and feeling grounded while doing so. As has been suggested, this can only be achieved by releasing what the past previously claimed as truth. Only by detaching from the security of an old truth can a renewed sense of safety manifest. Practicing ENM was a very visceral process of making this exact shift: of initially feeling completely lost and destabilized, only to eventually find footing in the safety of the now through the act of accepting a new reality. In this particular case, a reality that fosters love for more than one partner, that brings eye-opening awareness to co-dependency and jealousy by empowering autonomy, that dissuades falling into automation by building relationships upon the unique needs of those involved instead of a prescribed, uniform methodology that caters to the masses, assuming suitability for everyone.

It is difficult to articulate just how deep one must believe, honour, and practise this skill (because it is a skill) in order for ENM to work. Constantly bringing ourselves back to our present reality of a redefined relationship model and not allowing our judgement to be clouded by conventional standards is incredibly difficult. Fortunately, though, because relationships are a cornerstone to everyday human existence, that skill is exercised frequently and naturally becomes more and more instinctual. As a result of it being rigorously developed in the context of relationships, the skill of finding safety in the cyclical process of the present inevitably flows into other parts of life as well.

This may be what I miss most about ENM. The fluidity of moving through an unconventional process and the sense of freedom, empowerment, and accountability that comes with the responsibility of shaping something new and progressive. It keeps you on the brink of awareness at all times, fully conscious to what is relevant now because of its novelty. Unlike blindly following the instilled rules of monogamy that are so deeply engrained, you are forced to confront the unknown on a daily basis and create adaptable relationships (and a lifestyle to match) built on current needs, as opposed to an all-or-nothing relationship built on past and future expectations. It is near impossible to fall into unconscious automation immersed in these conditions.

I have since chosen to live a monogamous lifestyle, a decision that could have only been made genuinely having gone through my commitment (albeit temporary) to ENM. I actively chose monogamy from a clean slate by dismantling it, not from unconsciously falling into it. I essentially removed the compulsory piece, liberating it from its obligatory hold. Though, to this day, I often still ask myself: "Is there really such a thing as a truly liberated monogamous relationship, or does the very nature of exclusivity necessitate co-dependency?" I like to believe that I will empower myself to always co-create the relationship I want with my partner, whether I have one or more— through critical awareness, listening, and a robust sense of self. Somewhat paradoxically, it is this level of self-awareness that also allows me to be cognizant of the fact that some engrained beliefs may inevitably slip through the cracks. The power of the "relationship escalator" is a prime example.

One of the first things you will learn about when entering into the ENM world is what is known as the "relationship escalator." It is essentially a set of customary rules represented as chronological escalator steps that a typical monogamous relationship follows in order to achieve successful relationship status.[2] It begins with dating, then dating exclusively, then perhaps moving in together, then marriage, then solidified life enmeshment (family, schedules, finances), then procreation, culminating to a happily-ever-after family of 3+ living under one roof of a property you co-own with your exclusive partner. The term "escalator" is suggestive of two main factors: one, that the mark of a successful monogamous relationship is its ability to continuously move forward and upward via a linear trajectory where steps cannot be skipped or followed non-chronologically. And two, that there is no ability to go back. Once you are on the escalator, or in the relationship, it is *all* (a.k.a. moving forward and upward) or *nothing* (getting off the escalator). If you decide to get off the escalator, or out of the relationship, your only option is to start again. From the bottom. With someone else. Very prescriptive.

One of the most unhealthy qualities that monogamy breeds in relationships is this idea of all-or-nothing, or a very black-and-white perspective of right and wrong. The relationship escalator, for example, provides a set of clear criteria that determines whether or not a relationship is sound and therefore acceptable. It either is if you follow the rules of forward and upward trajectory, or it is not if you don't. "If we don't get married, then what are we even doing together?" "If we don't get married before we have kids, then what will people think?" "If I don't want to move in with him, then does that mean I am not serious about our relationship?" Welcome back the inevitable return of *if this, then that* binary thinking.

Not only do these rules ignore and invalidate the fact that human beings change (priorities, values, sexual preferences, career, heart and mind), but it impresses upon us the idea that if we deviate from the path carved out by those before us, the life we choose instead somehow loses viability, merit, or meaning. We are presented with only one right way to do things, and the power of individual choice is thus completely devalued and seen as something exercised by rebels and deviants. It is very telling of our culture that the word *deviant*, derived from the word *deviate*, meaning *to depart from an established course*, carries very negative connotations.

Fortunately, in this day and age, people are more accepting of those who reject the escalator—unmarried couples with children, partners who choose not to cohabitate, and of course, divorce. Admittedly, though, there is still a palpable underlying sense of judgement when people do not do what is expected. A reflexive questioning of *why* or *what's wrong* when an uncommon path is taken instead of a simple acceptance that that is the path they chose.

This is one of the most beautiful things that comes from ENM, just as it did from staying present in Portugal: the pursuit of realness. With no *shoulds* or *supposed tos* to hold us back or fabricate unjustified criticism, our authenticity, and our aptitude to see it in everyone and everything, reveals itself. We learn to accept things exactly as they are while also coming to terms with truly knowing both what we want and why. When I compare my behaviour on dating apps, for example, compulsory monogamy created stipulations—"Does he check all my boxes?"—whereas ENM sparked curiosity: "They seem interesting. Let's get to know them." The condition of "I accept you if . . ." stilted any way for authenticity to show up, whereas "I accept you as you are" welcomed it. When these same *if* and *should* conditions are stripped away from your beliefs and actions, only real reasons remain—reasons that are not inherited, standardized, nor societally-pressured, but simply the ones that are unique to you, now.

This level of openness is how we get to know ourselves and others in the most authentic way possible. It is how we are able to truly honour who we are in each evolutionary moment.

PART THREE : AS YOU ARE

Sometimes stepping into your power feels less like a triumphant entrance into the person you're becoming and more like a loss and abandonment of who you once were.

The final part of this book spans just over a year. It recounts a painful and regenerative chapter of my life—losing my mother in 2022 to becoming a mother in 2023. The importance of staying sharply present to a constantly evolving self, which also involved an especially introspective contemplation of persistent and informative dreams, became abundantly clear during this year. It was the only way I could get through it. As the last sentence of Part Two suggests, our authenticity squarely relies on this—our ability to accept and honour who we are in each evolutionary moment—to simply *be here, as we are.*

Creating Space

Creating space for the important things in life is something for which we all strive. That is sometimes easier said than done, depending on what those things are. Coincidently, this level of ease becomes irrelevant when you experience tragedy. Tragedy forces prioritization upon you.

My mom was diagnosed with endometrial cancer (cancer of the uterus) in 2020. She was quick to adamantly deny chemotherapy or any other kind of treatment. I know my mom never really processed nor healed from the passing of my dad in 2005, her loving and faithful husband of twenty-six years. She was profoundly lonely (her words). The toll of years of solitude, now dramatically amplified by the COVID-19 pandemic, were major factors in her choice not to pursue an arduous journey of cancer treatment. Though deeply saddened at first, I respected this decision. She continued to live her normal life with her diagnosis, looking and feeling great, so much so that sometimes I forgot she was sick. She held onto an unshakable faith (until the very end) that she would naturally heal her body through a remedy of healthy choices and positivity. It was actually quite inspiring to me; until its charm wore off and it wasn't anymore. Two years later, in June 2022, some seemingly minor leg pain prompted a doctor's visit, after which her health began to decline rapidly. Even though we all knew this day was imminent, it was still a surprise to me; a naively unexpected reminder that she had been sick this whole time. Then, her steadfast belief in "beating this thing," which she gripped onto so tightly and expressed so certainly, began to reveal itself as denial. The way she rigorously fought and evaded acceptance was the hardest part. She passed away shortly thereafter on August 27, 2022.

June to August were the hardest three months of my life. I often refer to this time as a "rollercoaster marathon," normally considered somewhat of an oxymoron, but in this case a very real depiction. I consider my mom's passing more difficult than my dad's for two main reasons. One, my dad's death was very sudden. I did not have to watch him unravel into someone I did not recognize. It was a gut-wrenching shock, not a gut-wrenching slow burn. And two, I was a numb shell of a person when my dad passed (his passing pushing me even further into this state). I was fully awake when my mom passed; fully attuned to my body, my emotions, my true self, thanks to all the self-actualization work I had done post-mental-breakdown of 2019. So, in hindsight, perhaps the two tragedies were in fact more equal than I consider them to be, but my lack of self-awareness during the first one caused me to feel it less.

For the better part of June, my mom lived at home with one of my three sisters or my aunt beside her. But after a number of emergency visits to the hospital due to severe leg pain caused by cancerous tumours pressuring her nerves, she was admitted to Riverview Health Centre for palliative care in early July. The next two months were basically a steady, emotionally charged period of prognosis chasing, doctor's updates, tracking constantly changing meds, digesting bad news, then good news, then worse news, sleep deprivation, and taxing schedule coordination. (My sisters and my aunt took turns staying with my mom so a family member was with her twenty-four seven. This was her firm request. She needed someone with her she trusted, as paranoia and hallucinations are a common symptom of the disease and are without a doubt intensified by the hefty daily doses of powerful pharmaceuticals.) All this, combined with the indescribable sadness and waves of hopelessness that I tried my hardest not to succumb to while watching my mom slip away, in agonizing pain, physically and mentally. All this, while trying to upkeep a sense of normalcy in life, wherever I could find it.

I tried to bring my work with me to the palliative healthcare centre when it was my turn to be with Mom. Some of her meds made her very tired, so she tended to sleep during the day and be up and (understandably) very agitated at night. I would bring my laptop and try to write this book, for example. Perhaps I genuinely thought I could get work done, or perhaps it was a subconscious effort to distract myself from what was happening. Whatever the motivation, it became abundantly clear that work was not getting done. Not only work, but recreational reading, puzzles, and trivial items on my to-do list that I thought I could do from my mom's bedside while she slept were impossible to accomplish. This was the point in time when I was forced to confront, face to face, the concept of creating space. This idea of making room for simply being instead of trying to fill it with constant doing, the subject matter of this very section. This abruptly necessary and important ability that involuntarily manifested for me as a consequence of tragedy must still be learned and developed in its absence. It is, however, our human tendency to do the opposite.

As you can imagine (or maybe you can't), watching the most consistently loving and reliable person in your life, the one who raised you and gave you life, fall victim to a disease that completely decimates her mind, body, and spirit forces you to stop; to instinctually, without question, stop. It forces you to accept defeat and surrender to the situation you find yourself in, to say "No, I can't" to everything that is not the thing that is currently consuming you. The things she would say to me as she uncontrollably slipped in and out of lucidity, as I watched her endure a fear and pain so raw and relentless; my heart will forever break from these haunting memories.

There came a time where I had no mental or emotional capacity to do anything other than just sit there. Even just sitting there felt like an unfathomable task. But I listened as best I could to the inner voice telling me to do so. I now know that that voice, the one that implored me to just be here, as I was, was the voice of intuition. It was the language of the present, of flow, that was earlier introduced in Part One.

Having endured something that I wish on no human soul, I am still grateful for what I learned. I have since made a very conscientious effort to create space in all aspects of my life; to make room for intuition, always. While it may have been during a time of tragedy, when grave misfortune did the work for me, that I began to hone in on this capability, it is the hard self-work that I presently commit to every single day that sustains it. In the slow-burning survival mode of losing my mom, I had no choice but to slow down and listen. But it is now an active choice I make regularly. Now, I make way. I make room. I accept and trust things exactly as they are without trying to apply outside pressure or intervention to them; to change or make them better. I allow the space I have created to speak for itself, to make way and room for intuition. As contextualized in my previously mentioned waterslide dream: to *widen the waterslide that is our purview, and to repeatedly prime our own channels of present awareness with the water that is trust in order to receive intuitive messages with which to align ourselves.*

There was another instance a few years ago where I am certain intuition was speaking to me. It was during a creative act. Granted, creativity is a much different experiential space than tragedy, though the one thing they do share is crucial to intuition: acute presence.

When I draw, I am acutely present. Especially when I sketch. Making quick, instinctual markings on a page, the act of which begins to reveal concept and form on its own, requires you to flow moment to moment without much forethought or prediction. Being in the moment is key. For me, drawing is middle existence. I am fully present, centred squarely between past and future. My ability to access both physical and metaphysical worlds is heightened. If you don't believe me, read on.

I was designing a tattoo for a friend. It was a commemorative tattoo for her grandma. With no specific reference images provided, her only request was for the design to include a sparrow, a clock, and some flowered branches, as all three were personally symbolic to her. Aside from including these three specific things, I had free reign over the final design.

I remember working on it, approaching it with little planning. Unlike many of my other tattoo designs, I did not have a vision of what it would look like in the end, as there was no request from my friend to make it look a certain way. I was not working toward something in particular. I remember it turning out very well. I remember finishing the piece and being very happy and satisfied with the results, my friend sharing these sentiments exactly. After inking the tattoo, she expressed how excited she was to show her grandma this piece of body art she had gotten in her honour.

A few days later, my friend sent me a photo along with a message saying she had recently visited her grandma to show off the new tattoo. The photo depicted her grandma sitting in an armchair in front of a dresser with an antique clock on it. The message read: "Take a look at the time on the clock behind her. It's been stuck like that forever."

I did not believe what I saw at first. Both the real clock in the photo and the one I had drawn in my friend's tattoo (the one for which I had no reference images nor design criteria) read 1:32. Not 1:30, not 1:35, 1:32. I had an infinite number of options when deciding what analogue time to draw on the clock in the tattoo, but for some reason my imagination had aligned with reality. You can find both the photo and the drawing in the appendix.

This is unexplainable, other than the inkling that the act of drawing opens a kind of metaphysical channel for me. It is really more than an inkling, though. I truly believe any creative act has the ability to connect us to a transcendent world beyond three-dimensional reality, because creativity, inventiveness, and imagination require complete presence, and complete presence is a pathway into the mystical. It makes sense then that tapping into deep presence (in this case, via creativity) grants us access into intuitive wisdom we would otherwise not be privy to. It is enchanting to consider the wealth of insight we can acquire simply by staying awake and present to each moment—moreover, realizing what we could be missing out on when we do not.

As we know, presence is expansive. Presence requires space to permeate. It cannot be compacted into a convenient timeframe, nor rushed in anticipation for the inevitable future, nor hastily stopped when the discomfort of true reality sets in. It is up to us to create the space for presence to not only exist, but to take command. It is only then when we experience the most clarity and richness.

As an artist, I see this manifesting in my practice all the time. The quality and authenticity of my work is directly reflective of how much space I give myself to create. When I allocate too many parameters or limitations to my artwork, it shows. If I tell myself I have to finish a piece by a certain time, it does not allow for intuitive creativity to unfold naturally. It puts control onto something that cannot operate well under such demands. To force something to be complete within a specific time robs it of its own blossoming process of organically becoming. I am grateful that I have my art to show me this firsthand, acclimatizing my awareness to see it manifesting in other areas of my life.

Creating space is about aligning yourself with the pace of the present. It is slowing down and noticing the power that comes with that. Naturally, this occurs in cycles. Recognizing and honouring the multitude of ways these cyclical experiences show up in life ensures that creating space is sustainable.

Honouring Cycles

I have come to wholeheartedly understand and appreciate that all life occurs in cycles, though it is difficult to have this perspective when we feel detached, separate from life itself. This "othering" from life occurs when we are conditioned to correlate success with external attainment, when we are hyper-focused on the destination of future goals more than the present journey, or when we view life and time as linear as opposed to cyclically regenerative. I believe it is the level of connectivity we feel (or lack thereof) that affects our ability to sense these cycles.

We forget all too often that we are part of nature. Just because our daily activities are ruled by machines within man-made environments, we are not exempt from existing in a world governed by natural forces. Yes, we live in an age and culture that is dangerously withdrawn from the Earth, the wild, and the very essence of humanity, but we must not let that obstruct our perception of the natural cycles that as yet persevere. Just because we cannot see them—or more accurately, are ignorant to them—does not mean they disappear nor have any less power over us. To become intentionally aware and conscientious of life's cycles is not only how we invite reconnection, but also a deeper understanding and appreciation for life itself. From the inhale and exhale of each moment, to the rising and setting of the sun each day, to the reoccurring lessons we forever unlearn and relearn, to the raw beauty of life and death, everything is reiterative; everything is regenerative. Life is not visualized as a straight line with a distinct past, present, and future, where the past is dead and gone as we move forward, but is instead revisited through progression, regularly returning us home in a cyclical manner. With this perspective, we feel part of and connected to something greater. Something beyond a material world where existential being relies on physical tangibility. The bigger, collective picture comes into focus, and singular, trivial matters become less relevant. Our commonalities and shared experiences outshine our differences.

The months following my mom's passing were obviously very difficult. They were made more manageable, however, by this knowledge of our inherent connection to nature's cycles. How comforting it is to see death not as an exodus, as something to be lost and never again recovered, but as the beginning of a new cycle. The inhale after the exhale, or the inevitable return of spring after every harsh winter. Honouring these cycles reminds us of our collective oneness and helps us find our way back home within each evolution.

I have always believed that our dreams are a way of returning home, of reminding us of who we really are. They truly are a transition from the end of one cycle to the beginning of another, a space that connects the previous night to the following morning. In sleep, our bodies are anchored in the present while our minds have the ability to visit an immersive metaphysical realm where we can relive past memories, see into the future, and imagine new realities. Dreams are a reminder of our connection to nature, to our instincts and intuition.

After my mom passed, my dreams were filled with reoccurring symbols. Some symbols, like water, were already familiar to me. I had previously dreamed of big bodies of water, floods, the ability to breathe underwater, and, of course, waterslides, to name a few. I knew the different ways in which water could be interpreted in the context of these dreams, which left me with satisfying revelations and an understanding that I had processed a subconscious blockage each morning after. There were two new symbolic images, however, that presented themselves only after her passing. I dreamed of these two things often; sometimes separately, sometimes together. Fire and hummingbirds became recurring main characters in my nightly visions.

After multiple dreams, some thoughtful research, and trusting my instincts, I came to the conclusion that in my dreams, fire was representative of intuition and hummingbirds were a representation of me. This brought a fascinating clarity to many of my dreams, illuminating self-awareness.

During the weeks and months immediately following my mom's passing, I felt emotionally delicate, but also liberated. It was a strange, conflicting set of feelings that I was unable to identify at the time. Being such difficult feelings to navigate and integrate while consciously awake, I believe it was the reappearance of the hummingbird in my subconscious dreams that allowed me to articulate and process what I was going through.

Hummingbirds are precarious, agile, little creatures. Their essence beautifully encompassed my feelings of simultaneous fragility and freedom. My heart was both shattered and relieved when my mom passed. Three months can feel like an absolute eternity when someone you love is going through extreme pain and suffering. It is a relief when that tumult finally ends, despite what it means. The relief does not take away the agony, however. To have both relief and agony co-existing in your mind and body is inscrutable, and nearly impossible to process consciously. Dreams have the natural power to reconcile and heal.

Just like the relationship of self to hummingbird, pairing fire with intuition was another strong correlation for me. Like water, fire carries many meaningful interpretations in dreamscapes. For me, the presence of fire always seemed to symbolize an inner knowing, a secret knowledge, to which only I was privy. Regardless of the scene or story, the image of fire evoked a power of knowing something special, which I was internally urged to act upon. I have always been convinced that it is less about the content of a dream and more about the feelings you receive while dreaming that is important. This case was no different. Regardless of the dream's narrative, I always felt that same deep wisdom's call to action whenever fire appeared.

A very memorable dream I had that holds the same level of significance as the waterslide one involved a hummingbird that was *on* fire. A hummingbird appeared above me in a forest clearing, flying about normally at first, then all of sudden burst into flames. It became frightened and panicked. It began to beat its wings faster and faster in an attempt to put out the flames, which inevitably had the opposite effect, making the flames even bigger. The dream had no conclusion. I woke up left with this unsettling image of a hummingbird on fire, desperately trying to extinguish the flames that engulfed it, only perpetuating the life-threatening situation it found itself in.

As I came to realize during my mom's steady decline, intuition can show up unexpectedly, without warning and without trying. Its spontaneous appearance demands listening to, no matter what. I think the purpose of this dream was to solidify this notion. Intuition is one of those things that cannot be commanded (as I have expressed seeing time and time again in my art). It must be left to manifest on its own, not by us trying to control it or chase it down, which can only happen when we let go and situate ourselves in the right position. A position where it comes to us naturally, as opposed to us trying to capture it forcibly. This means *trusting* that it will come to you when you need it, that you will know what to do when it does. All that is needed from our side of the equation is to remain present and receptive to its arrival.

The hummingbird in the dream (me) tried to fiendishly control the fire (intuition). And understandably so. Something so formidable typically causes a fight or flight response—a fight against, a flight from, rarely a surrender to. When intuition presents itself so abruptly and unapologetically, without any conscious effort on our part, just the way it did in the palliative care centre as I sat quietly with my dying mother, we often don't know what to do, so we resist it. We try to distract ourselves, push it away, fan out its flames. While this may seem conflicting to what I just said a moment ago about trying to capture intuition, the implication is the same. On one hand we attempt to run away from it (flight), on the other we attempt to chase it down (fight). But regardless, in both cases, we are trying to control it through resistance. We end up a helpless hummingbird, unable to save itself.

It's like this: when we try to hastily summon intuition at our own will, we suffer. We are a hummingbird fanning the flames of the fire. When intuition comes without warning, and we try to silence it out of fear, we suffer. We are a hummingbird fanning the flames of the fire. Whether we are summoning or silencing, we are trying to control what should be left free. The only thing we need do is be present and listen; *to let intuition burn through its own natural cycle.*

So what would the alternative have been in the dream? For the hummingbird to realize the detrimental effect control has over intuition, to then allow the fire to engulf it completely? Perhaps that kind of admittance would have, in typical dreamlike fashion, miraculously put out the flames immediately. Perhaps the hummingbird's willingness to surrender to nature would have somehow saved it. While I do not know the possibility of that outcome, I do know I have had two similar dreams that suggest that that outcome is likely.

I had a vivid dream of a bear attacking me once. He had my forearm in its jaws, his frightening, fang-bearing face not a foot away from my own as I felt the imminent approach of death. I remember feeling eerily calm about the situation as I heard a voice tell me that all I had to do was surrender, to allow whatever was happening to happen, to basically allow this bear to rip me to pieces, and not fight it. As soon as I did that, the bear released my arm and casually strolled away.

Another, much less disturbing dream I had involved me having to haul around a ton of heavy textbooks in a backpack. I remember thinking to myself, *How the hell am I supposed to carry all of these books and still get to where I need to go?!* An eventual realization that the wisdom held within the books would still remain even after I let them go, even after I decidedly put them down because I could no longer carry the load, was very appropriate for the dream's timing.

The first dream of the bear occurred around the time I was in a difficult relationship, in which I was naively trying to change my partner (who aggressively resisted my attempts). The second dream, involving the backpack of heavy books, came to me five months after my mom passed. The dreams were at least two years apart but carried with them similar lessons.

There is an element of surrender that is synonymous with the flow of natural cycles. Not only synonymous, but necessary. A cycle does not exist without surrender. An inhale cannot exist simultaneous with an exhale; one must be released before the next can take form. Without surrender, there is no breathing, no flow, no circle, no cyclical renewal. All there is is a straight line made up of burdens we stow away and carry that evade our consciousness, forever remaining unrecognized and unprocessed. In my two dreams, these burdens were absolved through surrendering: one by accepting that we cannot control everything, and one by trusting that the important parts of our past will stay with us.

I knew I had to let go of the unhealthy relationship I was in, or at the very least let go of the need to control or change my partner. The bear in my dream taught me that it is only when you release the need to control the things you cannot that they finally release control over you. I also knew I had to let go of some of the all-consuming heaviness I carried with me relating to my mom's death. My second dream reassured me that letting go does not mean forgetting. Rather, it is a turning of the soil where the past nurtures what is to come next. It is the everlasting memory of the words held in the book's pages, even if the books themselves are gone.

Cycles are always at play. Without recognizing and honouring the ones in which we find ourselves daily, we come *out* of flow. No longer aligned with the cycle of the present, we remain stuck in a linear timeline that does not embody wholeness. The best way I can articulate this idea is through the following quote:

All of the time, all parts of you exist.

Presence is expansive, cyclical, and whole. Your multi-layered and multi-dimensional self is palpable here, and only here.

(I jotted down this quote in 2020, along with a number of other simple, short yet thought-provoking phrases. I turned twelve of them into an art series, which I entitled "INTEGRATION." You can find a handful of them in the appendix.)

The Act of Surrendering

Surrendering is natural. It is inherently crucial to all cycles. Because Western culture has strayed so far from this belief, surrendering can unfortunately feel *un*natural, something we resist. It can feel passive, careless, or like giving up, when in reality, surrendering is a very conscientious and deliberate act. It is relinquishing control with purpose.

During the summer months of 2022, when my mom was very sick, I had to press pause on writing this book. I did not know when or if I would return to it, but I did trust in the surrender of making that decision. I knew that release would allow clarity to eventually present itself because purpose is a natural consequence of surrender. Letting go of one thing leaves room for another to manifest.

This book was left untouched for over six months. It was a bit uncomfortable not knowing what would come of it, especially considering the time and energy already put in. But, as an expected result of the surrender, a natural, cyclical invitation back to writing presented itself in January 2023, when we received the exciting news that I was pregnant.

Losing a mother then learning you will become one within four months of each other certainly reignited my need to express through the written word. Stimulated by surging emotions—from joy to depression, blessing and loss—I knew that moving through this experience as presently as possible was the only way to survive and hopefully thrive. Reflecting on and recounting this year-long journey sparked the return to this book.

The act of surrendering was a skill I quickly realized I needed to master during this time. Experiencing the extraordinary physical, mental, and emotional shift that is pregnancy is one thing. *Stepping into* while simultaneously *losing* one of the most important caregiving, life-giving roles there is is beyond overwhelming. Surrendering to the moment, and the reminder to simply be here, exactly *as you are*, was integral to this undertaking.

I was simultaneously creating a life and grieving a life. A time when this dichotomy felt especially sharp was Mother's Day weekend—which also, coincidentally, marked twenty weeks of pregnancy, the official halfway point. I was fully aware of the emotional toll this weekend would have on my mind and body, but I also wanted to celebrate reaching the twenty-week milestone. The plan for the weekend was to spend quality time with my partner to honour our growing co-creation and to also thoughtfully peruse my vast collection of mom photographs. Like everyone else that day, the plan was to celebrate motherhood.

Unexpectedly, I got sick on the Friday. And not just a head cold, but an incapacitating kind of sick. As someone who seldom falls ill, it was a surprise; a very unwanted one considering the special weekend plans I had made. Unfortunately, I was unable to do any of it. Even sifting through photo albums was out of my means. It was upsetting and also curious as to why I would end up being so hindered during such an important, highly anticipated time.

That Sunday, I received a card from a friend. When I first saw the envelope with my name on it, my immediate feeling was dread. I was confident it was going to be a sad card—a "Thinking of you on your first Mother's Day since your mom passed" kind of message. Instead, it ended up being the very opposite, a joyous card wishing me a "Happy first Mother's Day!", complete with a cutely illustrated weekly timeline comparing the growing size of my expectant baby to that of various fruits and vegetables. The real-time shift I felt from the sorrowful moment a saw the envelope to the cheerful moment I opened the card perfectly sums up my experience of that entire weekend. A slew of conflicting emotions I could not seem to harmonize. It was confusing, erratic, and disorienting, all heightened by being physically ill.

Three days before Mother's Day weekend, I had a powerful dream, one that warranted written analysis in my dream journal, just like all the others mentioned thus far. The dream did not last long, nor was it overly complex, but it left a lasting impression. I watched a large group of birds fly through the air in unison. They dove in and out of a body of water, totally synchronized in flight, as if performing a choreographed dance just for me. I remember feeling completely overjoyed and surprised at the sight. In total awe, I succumbed to the moment, stood still, and simply watched.

I have no doubt that this dream was a symbolic premonition of sorts. A way of preparing me for Mother's

Day weekend, offering up a perspective that would help me reconcile those confusing, erratic, and disorienting emotions. (Of course, I did not decode the dream nor arrive at this level of clarity until well after Mother's Day weekend. Nonetheless, the delayed insight was well worth it).

I like to think that the birds represented the various parts of myself and the many emotions that were fervent that weekend. They bridged sky and water, weaving in and out of the two, seemingly connecting a mother in heaven and a soon-to-be-one on earth. The birds, the selves, the emotions were all interconnected, working in complete harmony. I surrendered to the intricate dance in front of me, simply watching it all unfold.

Perhaps that is why I got sick. And perhaps that is why the birds were able to harmonize. In the dream and in reality, I was forced to just sit and watch, to just be. To not resist, intervene, nor control. Just like the hummingbird dream, allowing nature to take its course, making way for the cycle of life to offer a lesson in surrender and acceptance.

Would it have been harmful for me to have celebrated twenty weeks? To have gone through photos of mom as planned? I certainly don't think so, but perhaps this is what I really needed at this particular time. To simply surrender to the dance of emotions in front of me, to let them navigate themselves, and for me to be in awe of them doing so.

In addition to moments of surrendering *to* during this time, there were plenty involving the surrendering *of.* Feelings of loss and abandonment take over during times of grief. I was grieving both my mother and a former (pre-pregnant) self, so I was receiving a double dose of both.

From experience, I can tell you that surrendering someone you once had at the same time as someone you once were is a disconnecting, out-of-body experience.

Looking back, during early pregnancy, despite my best intentions to stay present, I often found myself wanting to skip ahead to the birth of my child. I know this is not uncommon for soon-to-be-mothers, but there was more to this desire than just wanting to bypass the discomfort and nausea. It was more about reclaiming an identity that I felt I had lost.

As a fitness coach, I felt the physical limitations of my body deeply over the course of my pregnancy, especially during the first half when I was barely showing. My energy, strength, and stamina were being siphoned into something not yet tangible or physically perceptible. The sense of loss was so much greater than that of gain. There was emptiness. An empty hole left from my mom, made deeper by a loss of a former, more physically capable self. With this came an unanticipated dissolution of not being seen.

I had many reoccurring dreams during this time of loss; loss of other as well as loss of self. The first of the two reoccurring dreams always involved deep feelings of abandonment from my family. The specific situation was always slightly different, but the feeling of rejection was familiar and consistent. In each dream, I would find out that my entire family—mom, dad, and sisters—had made plans, or had already executed certain plans, without telling me. Once it was brunch, once it was a family trip, another time it was a game they played together without me. In each of these dreams, upon finding out that none of them cared to inform me about their gatherings, I felt completely excluded and alone, astonished at the fact that I was overlooked for these important events. The one that felt the most charged with emotion was the dream about the game. This one actually involved only my older sister and my mom. I found out that they had been playing a game that, for some reason, I had ownership over. I had evidently created it, so I had to be present whenever it was played. I remember uttering the word "stole" multiple times throughout the dream, accusing my sister of taking something from me without permission: "You stole this game from me. It's mine. And now you're playing it with Mom?!" Unlike the other dreams of this nature, when I awoke uncertain of the message these visions were relaying, I knew the reasoning behind this particular image asserting itself so pertinently into my consciousness.

The same day I had the dream, my older sister's mother-in-law and I were casually conversing about the experience of my pregnancy thus far, and more specifically the support I had been receiving. While reminiscing about the lead-up to my niece being born, she lovingly reminded me about the attentive care my mom had given my sister. Throughout my sister's entire pregnancy, my mom would make weekly deliveries of homemade bone broth, a slow-crafted, culturally significant, nutrient-rich, and comforting food. (My niece is now just over two years old, and I think they still have containers in their freezer, which goes to show the abundance of my mom's love.) This seemingly inconsequential daytime memory triggered something deep within me come nighttime—a subconscious resentment of my sister having a kind of motherly support that I would never have. It was an unrecognized hostility, so deeply yet unknowingly felt that, in the dream, it manifested into the vindictive act of stealing. It is fascinating how the cycle of living and dreaming can force the confrontation with painful, buried emotions. Too overwhelming to confront while consciously awake, our dreams provide guidance within a nourishing, transcendent space of rest and recovery.

During this period of major transition to becoming a mother myself, it was clear from these visceral dreams that the emptiness of losing my internal, former identity was compounded by losing an external guiding figure. Together, this is what induced the intense feelings of not being seen, which in turn prompted the dreams of familial exclusion and abandonment. 1) How could I be seen by someone who was no longer there? I was missing that key, guiding figure from whom I could learn; my original, nurturing teacher that would make this life-changing transition into motherhood just a little bit easier. 2) How could I be seen with no confirmed identity? I am no longer this version of myself, but not yet that version, so how can I be seen when I am in transition? I was in the in-between phase, the interstitial space, having not yet fully stepped into this new role as a mom. Hence, in this moment in my life, it felt as though there was no one to see.

The second reoccurring dream I had three nights in a row. I retreat to an isolated glass house for safety. From within its walls, I speak to my dad over the phone, I kick strangers out, and I have the ability to see out while no one can see in. I see this glass box as my body, where I instinctively retreat to find safety, but whose walls are fragile. The deceptive rigidity of its glass walls shields me from hurt but in reality could easily shatter. During such a massive transition, my body creates a false sense of security by resisting all the change that surrounds it. The walls are self-built for protection. Protection from the pain and fear of entering motherhood without a mother of my own.

It was only when I immersed myself into and accepted this phase of the self-actualizing cycle that I was able to decipher an important lesson from this dream and reinvent it in a way. I had learned to reframe the distancing feeling of being unseen into a positive one that signalled the imminence of transformation and growth. Instead of recoiling inward to somehow salvage past parts of myself, to hold on to what was, to what could have been, I encouraged myself to be vulnerable and venture outward, opening up to what was happening in the now.

The important lesson: I needed to surrender to the softer, motherly body I was inevitably becoming and, in doing so, dismantle the glass walls of protection and past. Perhaps a more appropriate word, though, is *transcending*, as opposed to *dismantling*. I say this because when I have the re-invented version of this dream today, one month before my due date, the glass house still stands, except I am now on the outside looking in. I don't see much, nor do I have much interest in investigating the interior. The house is covered in vines and is not maintained. I have even had versions of this dream where there is brick added to the walls. I find it interesting that the house still exists as is; the walls remaining rigid, even reinforced by brick, instead of reconstructed with more organic, softer materials.

Perhaps it is a reminder that certain parts of ourselves are never demolished, nor disappear completely—we just move beyond them. They exist silently, perhaps collecting dust or gradually being buried under the seasonal overgrowth in our mind, as we walk by, passing it on a newly blazed trail.

As the previous section about honouring cycles concluded, flowing with the cyclical present facilitates this. It sustains a whole and multidimensional self that bears many unforgotten layers while continuously creating new ones. The end of one cycle provides the footing for the next, for stepping into your *power of becoming*. You no longer see yourself as what you once were, but for all the things you are at once.

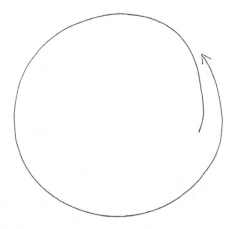

"AS YOU ARE"

Conclusion : Becoming . . .

I am currently less than three weeks away from my due date. It feels like the right time to be wrapping up this book, a project I started nearly three years ago with very little idea of how it would end or where I would be in life when it did. It is as if all the soul-searching that contributed to its creation has led me, fatefully and gracefully, to this particular place. A place of becoming and new beginnings.

I want to begin the ending of this book with yet another dream I had very recently. It was one that moved me in a particularly remarkable way. I believe it beautifully distills many of the pieces and lessons that make up my story, offering a level of illumination I did not know I needed, or thought was possible.

Up until now, since my mom's passing, I have had dreams of her, but she has never been the centre of attention. In my dreams, she is often around—her presence felt—but she is never the focal character. Much like during waking hours, she is omnipresent, hanging out in the back of my mind. In this particular dream, though, it was just the two of us. We were cohabitating in the house I grew up in, except it was present day.

I had just arranged all of my belongings very neatly on the second floor. I recall the great sense of satisfaction I felt by organizing my furniture. I proceeded to make my way downstairs to the kitchen, opening the door to the fridge in search of sustenance. The fridge was very sparse, except for a few morsels of old, dirty food, some of which had flies buzzing around them. The kitchen counters were similar, unkept and discoloured, a stark difference to the state of the clean second floor from which I had just come.

I found my mom tirelessly scrubbing the counters, bent over and determined to remove the dirt and stains. She turned to me and said, "Zeph, I worry that I will never be able to find myself again," referring to her state after the passing of my dad. She continued, "I worry that I cannot unlink my identity from your father." I remember feeling taken aback by her willingness to open up and share her grief with me. I proceeded to respond gently with follow-up questions and requests for elaboration on how she was feeling. A tremendous amount of connection, sympathy, and compassion grew within me as we conversed, and as she continued to habitually and mercilessly scrub the counters.

"This is what I do all day" was the next thing she said to me. "I wake up, and I clean. That's all I do these days." An overwhelming guilt and sadness then came over me. It was so strong that it permeated into the real world from dream world, and I woke up incredibly upset, crying in bed. I immediately got out of bed to put the dream into my journal.

I wrote down the details of the dream just as I have done here, tears still streaming down my face. As I began writing the word *guilt*, my hand took charge, as if, for a fleeting moment, my body detached from my brain, and I wrote the word *gift* instead, accidentally. I found this otherworldly, strange, as *gift* had become a very relevant word to me over the last few weeks. It was no coincidence that this word appeared seemingly out of nowhere as I was writing and reflecting about the feeling of guilt . . . .

I was deep in therapy at this time, moving steadily through the grieving process, even beginning to approach some semblance of closure. The one-year anniversary of my mom's passing had very recently come and gone, coinciding with her internment (the lowering of her ashes into the ground, next to my dad). This event was undeniably liberating, like the heaviness of her urn was removed from my heart and returned to source. It was a much-needed and important release—one that I would soon learn was deeply entangled with another: the release of *expectation*. (Something I have outwardly scrutinized frequently throughout this book.)

Over the course of therapy, I had come to discover that I associated *expectation* and *obligation* with my mother. As such, I believed the release and reframing of their meanings—as in my subjective interpretation of their definitions and the impact they had on my life until this point—was crucial during this alchemizing time in the grieving journey. It was a daunting self-prescribed task that I was committed to working through.

I had always viewed expectation and obligation as negative; something forced and pressure-inducing. Having also always associated them with my mother, holding myself accountable to loved ones was often their objective: *I am expected to fulfill this obligation that has been put upon me, over which I have no choice, because **I should be** accountable to the people I care about.* In deconstructing these two words, attempting to remove their hostile power and redefine them as something more resonant with my healing self, I began to willfully see them in a more positive light, more as autonomous invitations to be open and vulnerable: *I am expected to fulfill this obligation that I have chosen because **I am** accountable to the people I care about.* While both scenarios have the same objective, their reasons are completely different. The former scenario demands from a past-informed or future-driven, external voice, while the latter invites from a present, internal one. One produces guilt that distances self and other while the other is a gift that connects them. This profound reclamation, that of expectation and obligation being rooted in internal desire (*I am*), not external pressure (*I should be*), was unfolding concurrently with the dream of my mom and I in the kitchen. It was as if a long-awaited open dialogue between maternal generations was the antidote in moving forward, into seeding a refreshed set of beliefs and values about expectation for my new family upon laying an old family to rest.

There is a quote from a sitcom I frequently watch that effectively encapsulates this metamorphosis. This quote very much served as a beacon for me. In this sitcom, a group of close friends gather at Christmas, some of whom buy gifts for the other members of the group, while others do not. One of the grumpier friends of the group expresses his frustration with the act of buying gifts for others. His opinion is that buying gifts creates the obligation for everyone else to reciprocate. Another of the more generous friends responds discerningly with, "It's not the gift that is the obligation, the obligation is the gift."[3]

For the vast majority of my life, I have had the same mindset as the grumpy friend in this scene. A combination of my upbringing, societal conditioning, culture, ethnicity—down to the type of education and relationships I have found myself in over the years—shaped my view of expectation as a forced compliance, authoritatively implemented by one, rather than a shared, mutually respected agreement among all. Identifying and leaning into this shift in definition has been nothing short of revelational—and, even more so, rehabilitating. This most recent dream is proof of that. Though completely reluctant to do so in real life for eighteen years, my mom is finally open about the pain of losing my dad. The guilt-inducing expectation to protect and be strong for her daughters is released and replaced by an invitation; a long-awaited act of vulnerability that gives me permission to do the same. The expectations between mother and daughter no longer driven by *guilt (I should be)*, but by the *gift* of being vulnerable with one another *(I am)*. Whether it is mother and child, lover and partner, or two complete strangers, a *self* can only truthfully relate through this internal choice, to be present and vulnerable with *other*. It is as if through this last year of pain and grieving, questioning and processing, and being still and feeling, that the truth about the power of vulnerability was able to present itself in a very personal and moving way, through a dream (a common teaching vessel for me, and a way I also choose to believe my mom speaks to and heals me from the beyond).

This dream, along with much of the content of this book, provides an offering: ***vulnerability is powerful.*** Vulnerability connects us. It dissolves the rigidity and assumption of expectation (*I should be*) and replaces it with grace and autonomy by giving power to the present self (*I am*). When we are willing to be vulnerable with each other, to consistently show up presently, openly, and honestly, we willfully summon others to do the same, to reciprocate. Vulnerability is, therefore, also authenticity. It is the way in which we courageously allow others to see the truest, most raw version of ourselves.

Cycles rule this type of raw expression. Change and evolution, reframing and redefining, are intrinsic to authenticity. This concept is initially raised in Part One, where it is proposed that clarity requires *regression before progression*, or *unlearning then relearning*. Visually, this is the elemental design of a circle (or cycle). This kind of cyclical clarity allows us to continuously reframe and redefine our beliefs and ourselves based on an ever-evolving, present being, as opposed to an immutable one stuck on an unadaptable linear trajectory that unconsciously heeds past and future. This is how I transmuted *expectation* and *obligation* from *guilt* to *gift*. This is what I see as the cyclical art of becoming, which relies on our commitment to vulnerability.

It is sad because I believe it is our natural state and human right to be vulnerable. It is how we come into this world, born naked, exposed, and honest. But with age and life experience comes the belief that this a temporary and naive way of being; that somehow age and life experience makes you over-qualified to live in this way. It disallows you from remaining so open, as if you are no longer eligible to live so unprotected and unarmed. You learn to erect walls around a predetermined persona, as if the magnificent chaos of life warrants shielding yourself from the unknown instead of feeling every bit of it. Upholding this self-imposed state of rigidity then makes the cyclical art of becoming ever more impossible, for how is something expected to grow and regenerate if it is not allowed to be exposed to the elements?

Becoming relies on vulnerability, which nurtures authenticity. Upon finalizing this collection of thoughts, this introspective retelling of the past four years of my life, I realize that this book's aforementioned offering requires an important addition: *vulnerability is powerful **and sustains our stories of becoming***. For me, the story started with a simple commitment to staying present and culminated with me accepting and fully stepping into my power of becoming a mother. This journey, this cycle, this process of becoming is one that I suspect repeats itself over and over throughout a lifetime; three pivotal facets of which are revealed through each part of this book: *"BE," "HERE,"* and *"AS YOU ARE."* And so the story goes . . . .

My devotion to flow and presence is what ultimately compelled me to write this book in the first place. Exploring the interconnected meanings of clarity, trust, flow, intuition, and purpose beckoned the inaugural grounding reference point of what it means to simply and presently *"BE."* (The dot.)

"HERE" contextualizes this present being among past, future, physical, and metaphysical worlds (diagrammatically expressed with the addition of the crossed lines emanating from the dot). This contextualization makes deep self-awareness inescapable, for it situates you within our actual human existence. In learning the difference between internal and external motivations, you begin to uncover your own powers in the midst of social norms, noticing the difference between representation and actual truth. The binary dogma of good and bad, right and wrong, black and white, become ever more apparent, as well as unattractive and irrelevant. The realization that the binary or one-size-fits-all logic is a societal condition, not a human one, liberates us from being defined by these representations and empowers us to discover our own unique truths. We are called to blaze individual paths from a present and authentic perspective instead of planning them out from a future one using pre-existing blueprints, as if drafting a projection for life.

You need not forecast a path for yourself. You do not need to select from a binary list of available causes or steps that will get you to desired effects or outcomes. It is much simpler than that. All you must do is align with *middle existence, here, the present*, with what is most authentic and real to you in the now. The rest will follow naturally, without much effort at all. While the future self is too often the one we reference and idolize, it is actually the present one that will get us to where we need to be, for that is where our true powers lie.

"AS YOU ARE" is the chapter that challenges you to be vulnerable, to recognize and surrender to the natural, cyclical forces of life. Sometimes, this surrender is out of your control, forced by an external and fierce circumstance—like, in my case, tragedy. Other times, this surrender must come by choice. Voluntary or not, surrendering to the powers that be, to the situation at hand, is how the cycle continues and how the process of becoming progresses.

It is important to remember that surrendering to the powers that be comes after discovering your own. You are not just passively and unconsciously free-floating in this process of becoming. You are doing it with purpose, rooted in self-awareness. Like a tree, being *here* is being rooted in the earth; radically understanding through genuine curiosity and critiquing what we value at our core, what grounds us. This sense of stability is what allows the wind—the situation at hand, the powers that be—to dance through our branches without completely uprooting us. It allows you to be *as you are*, free, vulnerable, authentic, existing.

Preparing my mind and body for giving birth has brought unprecedented meaning to all of this. Birth is an absolutely phenomenal experience with practically zero predictability, a life-changing event where **being here**, grounded in your birthing intentions and affirmations, **as you are,** with flexibility and acceptance of whatever happens, is vital. It is literally and metaphorically life-giving. It is an undertaking for which I feel especially ready.

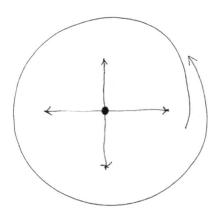

"BE HERE, AS YOU ARE"

This is where the story closes, though it should not be misconstrued as an ending. For as we have (hopefully) come to learn over the course of my musings, everything aligns with, is united by, and is ruled by cycles, and cycles have no definitive end.

Being present is well worth the dedication. Even so, we are bound to slip out of this state and regress into old patterns that hinder our clarity. We are human, after all. And that might be the most important thing of all to remember: that this is precisely the point of the journey. That it is, in fact, our humanness that takes us through the cycle of transformation, affording us the opportunity to constantly evolve. Rather than epitomizing growth as striving to transcend our human fragility, it is actually our willingness to confront these imperfections that perpetuates the momentum for growth. Honouring our humanness returns us home, brings us full circle each time we reinvent ourselves, and is the most honest way of becoming.

My biggest fear in life is to become unconscious. I hope to never fall into an automated existence where living means carelessly moving through a mindless routine. Fortunately, I think by trusting in the cycles that make up this life, we remain forever awake to them. We honour and cherish our ability to continuously reinvent ourselves within an evolving, cyclical process of becoming. In doing so, we resolutely avoid the monotony and limitations of following a linear path and are forever stepping into a newfound power.

To make life one giant flow state is to be eternally immersed in the process of becoming. So, I suppose my chosen purpose has been realized, and will continue to be, many times over, so long as I am present.

Your sole purpose in life is to show up,
fully present and fiercely authentic,
to each and every moment.

Appendix

Zephyra Vun

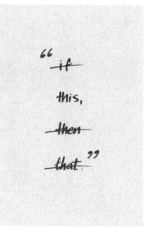

Blank Pages for Thoughts

Endnotes

1   Dr. Joe Dispenza, *Becoming Supernatural,* (Carlsbad, California: Hay House, Inc., 2017), 61–64.

2   Amy Gahran, *Stepping Off the Relationships Escalator,* (Boulder, Colorado: Off the Escalator Enterprises, LLC, 2017), 19.

3   Tristram Shapeero. "Intro to Knots". Community. Season 4, Episode 10, NBC, 2013.